"Ya, Ya!... Those Were the Days!"

by Bob Becker

Illustrations by Debra Harstad

Nostalgic Tales of the Past

Printed 1993
In the United States of America
by WHITE BIRCH PRINTING, INC.
Shell Lake, Wisconsin 54871

ISBN 1-885548-01-X

To order, contact:
BOOT PRINTS
701 College St.
Spooner, WI 54801
Phone (715) 635-2317

Dedication

"To old times...
and old-timers everywhere!"

Foreword

I come from a long line of old German storytellers.

As best I can determine, my ancestors — names like Becker, Weiler, Kemen, Frederick, Wallrich, and Faber, emigrated to America in the middle 1800's, settling in southeast Wisconsin. Why they came, no one's ever told me. But I suspect their reasons were typical of the wave of immigrants who left Europe in those times; political and religious turmoil, a desire to own land, the promise of freedom, an opportunity to build a better life in a new land.

They were people of the soil, farmers, as best I know. Folks who lived simply, believing in hard work, self-sufficiency, and minding one's own business. And those ethics and values were handed down, generation to generation.

Such was the cultural atmosphere into which I was born. My first memories, as a boy in the 1930's, revolve around farm life; of horses and cows, barns and windmills. And the people who lived there; my parents, grandfathers, grandmothers, uncles and aunts.

Life was uncomplicated. Electricity hadn't yet reached out into the rural areas. Television wasn't even a dream; radios, crude crackly, battery-operated sets, poor at best. Even the written word was sparse, limited to weekly newspapers and occasional magazines.

People communicated by talking.

Well I remember the Sunday afternoon get-togethers. Kinfolk would come to rest on lawns in the shade of tall trees, or to gather around long oilcloth-covered kitchen tables, to visit.

There the stories would flow, of by-gone days, of good times and bad, of people...friends, neighbors and relatives. Tales, spiced with humor and laughter. Others serious, poignant. And when the afternoon wore down, and the time came to "start the chores," to milk the cows and feed the chickens, a final story would always be told.

As the teller's last words fell on his listeners' ears, a pause, a hush, would settle over the group, as they reflected on what he, and others, had said. A slow rustle of feet, the scraping of chairs, would sound.

And somewhere from the midst, a voice would softly say,

"Ya ya! Those were the days!"

Acknowledgements

These stories were written as newspaper columns from 1986 to 1993, and are included here as they originally appeared. In some instances, time and other circumstances, including deaths, have since altered the settings.

My heartfelt gratitude goes to the many people who allowed me to enter their lives and to write about them. And to the editors and publishers who accepted and published these tales.

To my wife, Marian (Momma in the stories), I extend special thanks for the help and counsel contributed by her.

The Author

Contents

The Old Place

The set of buildings had been built well before the turn of the century. My folks always called it "The Old Place." There they lived when I came into the world back in 1927.

The old farmstead laid on a south slope along a gravel town road — just past the bridge that crosses the little creek which meanders along the barnyard on its way toward Lake Michigan.

There was a big red barn for the cattle and the horses; a machine shed, blacksmith shop, pigpen, some corncribs, a milkhouse with a tall windmill standing over it, and a modest white clapboard house.

And there my first memories were etched deep into my brain.

I remember those long-gone days well. The hay mows where I played in sweet-scented timothy, the fields I roamed. The big green lawn where I sat under maples and burr oaks and watched the steamers plying back and forth on the horizon of the big lake to the east, all the while wondering how its water could seem higher than the land.

I remember the old house with its back porch and summer kitchen. And inside the door, the main kitchen where my mother baked her loaves of golden bread in the oven of a black, flat-topped, silver-handled, wood-fired cookstove. There, on cold winter nights, I watched by kerosene lamp, the lacy, fern-like frost patterns slowly creep across the single-pane windows. In the mornings, the dipper in the water pail would be frozen tight.

I went back a year ago, about now. Visiting the relatives, I took a couple hours and drove out to my birthplace. I asked Momma to go along. I wanted her to see some of my roots.

I knew the place had changed. Someone had told me years ago that the house had burned. But I wanted so badly to once again touch the earth I'd walked as a boy.

I found the driveway and parked the car. I'd go alone. Momma would stay in the car sheltered from the cold northeast wind blowing in from the lake. Besides, it was better that I go by myself, alone with my thoughts.

I looked up, and there, nailed to a gnarled two-foot oak, I saw the sign. *"No Trespassing"* it said, and I paused. But the emotions boiling inside me were overpowering. "I was here first!" I told myself and without a twinge of guilt, I headed up the narrow lane.

The house, the barn, all the buildings were long-gone, I could tell. Yet, as if yesterday, I could see each and every one of them. And then I noticed the pine seedlings. The calf pasture had been planted to shiny green white pines.

I walked on to where the windmill had stood. Now, only a two-foot well casing protruding from the ground remained. On past the blacksmith shop where, at a so-tender age, I had sawn down my grandfather's hog-hanging tree, almost taking down the windmill and almost killing myself.

Ahead, to where the machine shed and the horsebarn had been, I slowly moved, then out behind the cowbarn where the wooden-staved silo had stood. There I found the gray, weathered, fieldstone foundation, and I rested my foot on the old wall and gazed at the brush and weeds that almost hid the gutters where my father hand-milked his cows by lantern light.

I turned to look out over the cow pasture, and I saw them again; rows of pine seedlings and spruce with, here and there, black walnuts poking toward the sky. "How can it be? Who would plant a forest where ranch homes should be sprouting?" I thought.

I retraced my steps and found the weed-covered foundation of the old house. The memories flooded back. Somehow it seemed smaller than I remembered. Yet there had been the livingroom, the parlor, the bedroom.

With the cold wind cutting my face, I turned across the old lawn to the car. And there they were once more, the little pine seedlings. Even the lawn had been planted.

I'd done the right thing, I knew. As I silently headed the car back to town, I felt better. I'd gone back to the Old Place, and I'd spanned those sixty years.

And I'll go back again. And when I do, maybe just by chance I'll get lucky. Maybe I'll find the present owner there. And if I do, I'll introduce myself and shake his hand. And after a bit, I'll tell him tales of years gone by. Perhaps my words will add something to the legacy of the land he now owns. Maybe he'll listen and even thank me for stopping by.

I hope that happens. You see, there's an old forester that wants very much to thank him — thank him for planting those trees.

Country School

Springtime in a country school. The Hillcrest school stood at the corner where the town road that passed our farm met the state highway. It was there that I began the first grade on a September morning back in 1932, carrying an Eight Brothers tobacco pail filled with thick homemade bread sandwiches, lined with scrambled eggs. It was there eight years later that I graduated from the eighth grade, a big milestone for country kids in those times.

The old school is gone now, a victim of progress. The narrow concrete highway had to be widened. That took a chunk of the front yard. Besides, its two rooms had outlived their day, and it was replaced with one of those modern, rambling, one-story jobs a mile to the north.

I drove by the site recently, now just a vacant piece of ground. Unless you grew up in the neighborhood, you'd never suspect that a couple generations of farm kids got their basic education there.

And the old memories came flooding back. The "little room" where the 1-4 grade kids sat. The "big room" for those in grades 5-8. My two teachers, great teachers, Miss Ridge and Miss Lytle.

As I looked across the old school grounds, I could hear the voices of my classmates, the laughter, the play, yes the fights of a thousand recesses and noonhours. Springtime was the best I decided.

Spring was a time of release. Gone were the bulky mackinaws and four-buckle overshoes. Feet seemed to take wings as they touched bare ground again. Let the school windows be opened to bring in the first warm, balmy breezes; and even the teachers seemed to breathe sighs of relief. Recesses and noonhours turned loose an avalanche of pent-up winter energy.

Out would come the bean bags, the baseball mitts, the marbles and the jump ropes.

The bean bags would be first. Today they wouldn't be allowed, too dangerous. Made by our mothers of cloth sewed into six-inch squares, they were stuffed with beans or shelled corn. All of us boys had to have a bean bag! You haven't lived until you've been whopped a couple times alongside the head with a bean bag in a game of tag.

Bean bags got our baseball arms in shape, and as soon as our diamond in the cow pasture across the road dried out, there'd be the one school baseball and bat for games of "scrub" and "500" during the short recesses. The noonhours were different. Lunches would be gulped so that "sides" could be chosen for a real game.

Some of those farm girls could throw and hit a softball pretty good, and it wasn't unusual for the better ones to be picked ahead of boys with poor eyesight or coordination. And it wasn't unusual to have the teachers join in as spectators or arbitrators when a dispute over a close play at homeplate got too heated.

But then there was the marble shooting. For about two weeks when the frost was coming out, marble shooting was big. What happened to marble shooting? I haven't seen a kid playing marbles for years. It's too bad. You could learn a lot about people shooting marbles. Things like who's honest, who will cheat.

There were games of pot, little ring, big ring and chase;

and we prized our "steelie" shooters and our glass "puries" that we held up to the sun.

We weren't supposed to play for "keeps," but we boys did. Anyone that squealed to the teacher would do it only once. Like Harry Truman said, "If you can't stand the heat, stay out of the kitchen."

I recall a time when I was shooting real good, "skinning" my buddies to where I'd amassed a small fortune of forty-fifty marbles which I carried around in a leather pouch. One day I couldn't resist inspecting my winnings while the classroom was stone silent.

Well, I got careless and dropped those beauties on the floor. Now, you can't imagine what a bag full of marbles sounds like rattling and rolling around in a dead-quiet school room.

Miss Lytle peered down at me over her glasses from her desk and said, "Bring those up here!" I was out of the marble business.

And as I sheepishly returned to my desk, I can still see those girls hunkering their noses deeper into their notebooks, smirking and snickering.

The teacher's pets!

Old Jack

Old Jack was one of our farm dogs. Do people still have farm dogs? I don't seem to see as many as years back. Where I grew up everyone had a good farm dog.

A good dog was like a good hired man. Jack was one of those. He had his chores to do, and he did them well. Duties like helping to bring the cows home and keeping order amongst all the livestock around the place.

Take, for instance, a recalcitrant bull or a cantankerous boar pig that refused to take orders. All you had to say was, "Get 'em, Jack!" and he'd be swinging from that bull's tail or that boar's hind leg. There'd be the god-awfulest bellering and squealing that you ever heard.

Old Jack was respected from the smallest leghorn chicken right up to my grandfather's old gray riding mare.

But Jack was more than just the enforcer around the place. He was also what every farmer called a good "watch dog."

From his house under the elderberry tree, just off the back porch, he had a full view of the driveway and everyone and everything that came on the place. Everybody got a security check whether they liked it or not.

Back in those depression days there were a lot of men on the move. Tramps, hobos, bums; they were known by many names. Men looking for work or at the extreme, begging for a square meal.

Then there were the peddlers and junkmen. People trying to scratch out a buck by selling all sorts of odds and ends or buying scrap metal, old newspapers and rags. There were even a few chicken thieves around who weren't above hitting the henhouse in the dead of night.

So it was important to have someone around to keep an eye on things. And Old Jack was the best.

Let a peddler drive in the yard, and Old Jack would be the first to greet him, parking himself next to the car door with his 'hold it mister until the boss gets here' look. Talk about communication! No peddler ever misunderstood.

Old Jack knew his job and did it well.

That is, until that hot August Sunday afternoon when a family reunion was held. It was one of those country-folk affairs where the relatives come out from the city, everybody has a good visit, topped off with a big supper of fried chicken and old-style potato salad.

Now, I come from a long line of Germans. And you just didn't hold a German family reunion back in those days without a couple cases of that amber liquid that made Milwaukee famous.

The day was hot, everyone was socializing real good; and Old Jack, being a member of the family, was there too.

Well, as my Uncle Ted tells the story, someone poured a cold one for Old Jack. Now, Jack was thirsty so he gave it a try. Not bad; a little more body than the water in the stock tank; but then not bad. Besides, a dog of his stature didn't want to be a party pooper.

As the afternoon's festivities wore on, Old Jack got into the swing of things real good. A couple more cold ones, and you could say he had a real fun time.

And when the party broke up at milking time, Old Jack

wove a wobbly path back to his house under the elderberry tree.

Well, that night was a shameful thing. For the first time in his illustrious career, Old Jack was off duty. He was forced to call in sick, as they say.

That night, a hobo could have rolled a Bull Durham in the hay mow and burned the barn down. The chicken coop could have been emptied of Grandma's prize leghorns. And we kids could have been whisked from our beds.

The next day was a little better. Old Jack made it to his feet, but he was in a very ugly mood to say the least. Every fowl and animal on the place gave him a wideberth. And there were frequent trips to the stock tank to ease the throbbing pain in his head.

But a deeper hurt came from the terrible wound to his pride. His spotless work record had been besmirched.

Well, and my Uncle Ted swears it's true, from that day forward, all you had to do was wave a brown bottle in Old Jack's direction, and he'd curl back his lips, show his long white fangs and emit a deep-throated growl.

One trip through the never-never land of humans and one smudge on his career was all that Old Jack could stand.

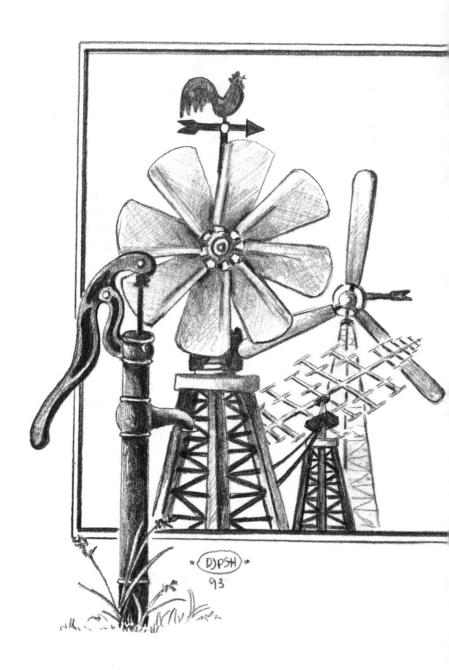

Windmills

I have this "thing," this affection for windmills.

The sight of an old windmill turning in the breeze turns my thoughts too, back to my boyhood days. Windmills are a nostalgic link to my past; a time when life was simpler — though not necessarily better.

As I travel around the country, I watch for windmills. Or, as in most cases, what's left of them. Like a team of horses pulling a wagonload of hay, you don't see many windmills any more.

A couple years ago I happened to be watching Johnny Carson. On the show, John had a guest, a 97 year old farmer from Iowa. The old gentleman was sharp as a tack; a real joy to listen to, to watch.

John and the old farmer had a great dialog going between themselves. And John asked the man what the most significant thing was that he had witnessed in his farming career.

When electrical power came, the man answered without hesitation.

The audience laughed with amusement. The old gentleman appeared a bit flustered. People were laughing at something that had been said in all seriousness.

And I understood. Unless one lived in the days before electricity came to rural America, one can't possibly appreciate the impact it had.

"Bob, go turn the windmill on," my grandfather used to say to me. And then, maybe an hour or two later when the stock tank was filled with water; he'd say, "Bob, go shut the windmill off."

In each case, over to the windmill I'd go. Pull the wooden handle attached to one of the mill's legs to turn it on. Release the handle to shut it off. High overhead the marvelous machine would start and stop. No switches, no electric motors.

In recent years I've gone back to both of my grandfathers' farmsteads. The windmills I knew so well are long gone. Yet I see them as clearly as yesterday, standing solemnly there by the milkhouse on their four galvanized angle-iron legs.

I can hear the purr of the many-bladed rotor spinning sixty feet in the air, the metallic clink-clunk music of the pump as it methodically pulled cold water from deep in the earth. And I can see the long, wide fan, replete with a few .22 bullet holes, holding the spinning blades firmly into the face of the wind.

The other day I was driving Highway 53 north of Solon Springs. There, off the road a bit, stood an old windmill; it's rotor merrily turning to the cold, brisk, northwest wind blowing across the stark, snow-covered farmyard.

And I stopped. I paused to watch. Was it pumping water? No, the pump shaft had long been disconnected. The mill was just there, there where probably it's stood for 75 years, there because no one has yet been driven to tear it down.

I looked. And I let old memories bubble back.

"Today I've got to oil the windmill!" my grandfather used to say to me. "Oh, boy!" I'd think. Oiling the windmill was exciting — for me. But gramp didn't relish the job.

Cautiously he'd climb the narrow steel-runged ladder up one leg of the mill's frame, a long-spouted oil can in his hand. And I'd watch as he gingerly raised himself onto the small, unguarded platform high in the air. There he'd stand, holding on with one hand, greasing the gear box with the other.

When once more he stepped down on earth, the strain of his effort showed on his face, in his deep breaths. For another six months the job was done.

Back in the early 1930's, when I was growing up, every farm had a windmill. You can still see their remains if you look close in the farming country. Southern Wisconsin and Iowa are great for windmill watching.

But it's rare to see one that still pumps water. Today, many sprout television antennaes at the top of their towers, their rotors and fans removed. And the sight of my old friends being prostituted to support a modern-day gadget tears me up a bit inside. Somehow it just ain't right.

Then some are still standing apparently just for sentimental reasons. Grapevines and ivys entwine in dense masses through their legs and cross braces.

Recently in Iowa, I saw a mill that was well-maintained, freshly painted. Yet, there spinning in the prairie wind, was its rotor painted in concentric circles of red, white and blue. Like a kid's pinwheel that you buy in the dime store.

But most are just standing, dying slow deaths, blades missing from their rotors, rusting and sagging.

I look at them all and I ponder the life they've seen. What a story each could tell! How many best sellers they could write.

My old friends are fast disappearing. And that's why I treasure them so deeply.

The Hog Hanging Tree

Working in the woods! I remember the first two trees I cut. Barely into grade school; maybe eight, nine years old, I started trailing along behind my uncles to my grandfather's woodlot on my Christmas vacations.

It was there with Uncles Bill, Ted, Joe, Amy, Vince and Allie that I learned to pull a cross-cut saw, drive a wedge and swing a double-bitted axe. Each fall my grandfather would saddle up his old gray riding mare and ride through his woods to blaze the trees he wanted cut come winter.

This was the 1930's. Gramp prided himself on running a self-sufficient farm. So "the boys," my uncles, would be dispatched each morning after chores, and the oaks and hickories would come down. The better cuts would go into logs for lumber around the farm, next would be fence posts, and last would be firewood to heat the huge twelve-room brick home.

Well, after hanging around the logging awhile, I figured I was ready to do some cutting myself. I pestered my uncles long and hard to let me cut a tree. Finally my Uncle Allie handed me an axe, picked out a little hickory; and said, "Here, have at it!"

Well, I beavered away at that little tree, never hitting the same spot twice; Allie, all the while, standing by to make sure I didn't beaver off a couple toes in the process.

Finally, the tree began to sway, and a last swing brought

it down with a soft thud into the snow. It wasn't much of a tree, but to me it was as good as a giant redwood. I'd done it! My first tree was cut.

The scene now shifts to my second grandfather's farm where I was born, and lived. A wonderful place with hay mows, machine sheds, horses, dogs and fields to roam.

But my very favorite place was my grandfather's blacksmith shop. If there was anything going on in the blacksmith shop, I was there. I'd watch fascinated as my grandfather worked his forge, heating a horseshoe to a bright orange; the sparks flying as he shaped the shoe on his anvil, listen to the "clang-clang" of his hammer.

Well, one day I was nosing around that shop when there, on the wall, I spotted a one-man crosscut saw. Now that was a saw for me, and I got up on an empty nail keg and took that saw down from the wall. I was right. That saw fit me to a tee. Now all I needed was a tree, and I could go back into the logging business.

I didn't have far to look. Right outside the door stood a gnarled old box elder, maybe eighteen inches through. It had a good lean to it, right toward the milk house and the windmill as a matter of fact. But that didn't bother an experienced logger like me.

It didn't bother me either that it was my grandfather's hog-hanging tree, the place where each fall at butchering time a couple of pigs were hanging high.

Well, I put that saw to that tree. Spurts of yellow sawdust squirted out with every pull. The lean of the tree made the cutting easier, and in no time at all the box elder crashed to the ground. I stood there proud of my handiwork. The tree was down; I'd barely grazed the milk house, and I'd missed the windmill entirely.

Now, the crash of the tree had sent one of those, "what's that kid up to now" shock waves around the farm, and in just a minute or two my grandfather came running up.

I'll never forget the look on his face, a mixture of fear and anger. Fear that I'd killed myself. Anger that his hog-hanging tree no longer existed.

He looked first at me standing there with the saw in my hands. I was in one piece. He looked at his milk house. Sure there were a few branches bent against one side. He looked at his windmill. That was still standing. Finally, he looked at the down tree.

The worried look on his face changed to one of relief, and a big smile creased his face. Once more he looked at the tree, then down at me and said, "It was rotten anyway."

And with that, he turned and walked away; still smiling, I'll always believe, in the satisfaction of the initiative his first grandson had shown.

He was that kind of a guy.

She Was A Rock

Her day will be coming up next week. She'll be eighty. I've known the lady for a good number of those years. But not as well as I should have.

I met her last summer at a family gathering, and I wanted to talk with her. So I pulled a couple lawn chairs into the shade of a big tree and asked her if she'd like to visit. And we talked.

I asked her about her health. I knew she was taking some medication. "Oh, about the same. Good days and not-so-good days," she told me. I thought she looked great and told her so; congratulated her for being active, for taking care of herself in the house she's lived in the past fifty years, the last thirty as a widow.

I asked about her family; her children, the grand-children, the great-grandchildren, the pictures of which rest in her livingroom, closeby for her to see.

And then we started talking about the old days, depression times back in the 30's when she was a young farmwife struggling to make ends meet. How it was to raise a family in an old farmhouse, to cook meals over a wood-fired range, to carry water from the windmill down by the barn.

Times were tough. Yet she was a rock, an anchor, in those troubled times.

She'd lost a son at an early age. Yet somehow she'd seen her other seven through grade and high school. And when each was handed their diploma, there would be a wristwatch waiting, bought with dollars she'd sacrificed to put away.

She watched as the seven, one by one, went out into the world; listened and encouraged as several talked of college. And, in time, they returned with five bachelor's degrees and three master's degrees. Three teachers, a nurse, and a renegade forester.

Oh, I knew quite a bit about her. But I wanted to know more. "What was life like back when you were a girl?" I asked.

And she told me about country schools, of muddy, rutted roads through the woods. How she and her brothers drove a pony hitched to a wheeled cart to school, a cutter through the snow in the winter. How the pony had to be unhitched and tied in a livery stable each morning when they arrived at school, and the process reversed each afternoon for the journey home.

I learned about bricks that were heated in the oven and placed under horse blankets draped over laps to fight off the winter cold.

How at Christmas time, her father would rise at three o'clock in the morning to feed and water a team of horses. How the family would climb aboard a bobsled for the trip to church for the five a.m. mass. How the cold air bit, the stars twinkled in the early morning sky, of sleighbells jingling across the still countryside.

She told me about old-time Christmases. Of trees, cut from spruces her father had planted, standing decorated in frontroom parlors. How candleholders were clipped to the branches to hold the burning candles. How her father worried about a fire.

"How did you dress back in those early days?" I asked her.

And she told me about long dresses, brown cotton stockings, of one-buckle rubber galoshes and high-button shoes. How she used a button hook to fasten the shoes.

"Tell me about the old cars," I said. That brought a hearty laugh. "Oh, those!" she smiled and went on to tell about her father's first automobile, a long-hooded Mitchell touring car with wooden-spoked wheels, leather seats and isinglass side curtains. How her father had driven all the way to town, six miles, in first gear the first time he took it out on the road.

She told how her mother was afraid to ride with him, thinking he drove too fast. How once he'd taken the corner down at the highway too fast, the gravel flying, and stammered, "B-B-By gol, Mary! I think we made it!"

The lady has lived quite a life her eighty years. From bobsleds to jetliners and rocketships to the moon. From party-line wooden telephones cranked to announce your "ring," to satellites bringing live pictures from around the world to her television today.

There'll be a small celebration next week. Some of the family will stop by, others will call. Maybe there'll be a ride to a quiet restaurant, a toast or two, some gifts to open. You can bet it'll be low key. That's the way she'll want it, you see.

Have a good one, Mother. Have a good one.

Red Bandanas

The red bandana handkerchief and I have been good friends for many years. I consider my old pal right up there with motherhood, the flag, apple pie, ice cream and baseball when it comes to things that truly represent what's American.

I grew up with the red bandana. In my early years, there were two kinds of handkerchiefs, the standard white one and my red friend. The white ones were reserved for special occasions like church, weddings and funerals. Old Red did the job the rest of the time.

My father, grandfathers and uncles all carried red bandanas around the farm. Those faithful red squares served many purposes beyond mopping sweaty brows and relieving congested nasal passages.

Many was the time one was tied across their faces at "thrashing" time to filter out grain dust, or wrapped around necks at haying time to keep chaff from sifting down inside a shirt to itch and scratch. And there were occasions too when a skun knuckle or sliced finger was bound up with Old Red.

The old-time western movies of that day all had a good sprinkling of bandanas. No self-respecting cowboy actor would be seen on the screen without one tied jauntily around his neck. It gave him that final touch of authenticity.

So it was natural that I would grow up falling in step with the red bandana's deep traditions. There're always two of them in my hip pocket for instance, when I'm working in my woods. I've never cut myself with a chain saw, but I've come close. And if I ever do, those two little red friends will be there to bind me up until, hopefully, I can get to a doctor.

And there've been a multitude of other uses. Things like marker and warning flags and sweatbands for my forehead. Many a time I've dipped one into a cold trout stream and tucked it under my cap on a hot afternoon. A piece of Old Red has even served as an emergency replacement for an ice-fishing tip-up flag.

More than once, I've hung one on a hazel bush to mark the spot where a grouse has gone down while I circled to search for the bird.

Yes, Old Red and I have had a long and good relationship.

Not so with Momma, however. She can't understand this friendship, and for thirty-five years she's been trying to wean me away from my old chum.

But I know where she's coming from. She's a city-raised gal you see, so how can she possibly understand good country culture? She's tried to get me to switch to blue and even blaze orange, but they have blah personalities, and I go on running around with Old Red.

I saw an ad awhile back in one of the big city newspapers for designer jeans. I was aghast that the belt was fashioned from red bandana handkerchiefs.

Well, you can forget that. The red bandana will never be at home in the chic circles of high society. Its roots go too deeply into the fabric of workingclass America, and it will always belong where sweat still drips and noses still run.

I don't know if there's a red bandana on display down at

the Smithsonian Institute in Washington, but there sure should be. And it should be right alongside the walking plow, the double-bitted axe and the long-handled shovel; the tools that did so much to build this country.

One of these nights when there's a Brewer game on, I'm going to cut myself a good-sized slice of Momma's apple pie, add a big scoop of vanilla ice cream, and settle down just as they play the Star Spangled Banner. I'm going to feel very American.

And you can bet that there's going to be a red bandana handkerchief there to wipe the crumbs from my mustache.

When Momma's not looking, of course.

Grandma's Gardens

I see people around the country putting their gardens in. I don't garden any more, but years ago, when the kids were small and we lived further south, we always had a big garden. It's a great way for a family to work and play together, and it's educational, too.

As a boy, I joined our neighborhood 4-H club. There wasn't much social activity for country kids back in those days, so what could I lose? Besides, there were a couple good-looking girls in the club.

Now, as everyone knows who has ever belonged to a 4-H club, you have to have a project. They didn't offer anything in fishing, so I chose gardening.

Oh, I put in the usual stuff — onions, peas, beans and carrots. But my specialty was watermelons.

I got pretty good at growing watermelons. And I want to tell you, it's a rich feeling for a country boy to stand in the middle of his very own watermelon patch and watch those green beauties grow and ripen around you. They were as good as money in the bank as far as I was concerned.

About the middle of August, I'd start sampling my crop. I got so I could select the ripest one every time after some trial-and-error thumping.

And what could be better than settling down under a cool shade tree on a hot August afternoon with your very own home-grown watermelon and a good sharp jackknife?

Ah, yes, talk about the good old days!

I got my first gardening training from my grandmother when I was, I suppose, seven or eight years old.

Every spring about this time, one of my uncles would give Grandma's garden spot a good shot of well-rotted manure and then disc and drag it until the soil was powder smooth and flat as a pool table.

When that was done, Grandmother would put on an old pair of bib overalls, one of those blue long-sleeved farm shirts and a straw hat, and if I was around, draft me to give her a hand.

At the time, I thought I was there to work. But in later years, I came to realize that she had another reason; I was the pupil, and she was the teacher.

Grandma immensely enjoyed putting in her garden; humming, smiling, and laughing. Perhaps it was the opportunity to get out of the house into the spring sunshine; a different kind of creativity; a break from the day light to dark chores that went into being a farm wife and a mother to six sons and three daughters.

Her garden was no rinky-dink hobby operation. It was a necessity, and the better part of it would end up at the end of the summer as long rows of blue mason jars on the shelves down in the fruit cellar; no small achievement, when one considers that the canning was all done over a woodburning cook stove.

These were the 1930's. There were no freezers. In fact, there was no electricity.

So, she'd send me down the rows with a stake with a big ball of binder twine wrapped on it. The rows had to be straight and spaced exactly the right distance. Then with her hoe, she'd make the trenches for the seeds and plants. All had to be planted precisely the right depth and spaced to grow to her high standards.

There were the usual vegetables — onions, radishes, peas, carrots, beets, leaf lettuce, tomatoes, lots of beans, and, of course, potatoes. I was baffled by the way the seed potatoes were sliced, not believing they would grow, but she explained how each slice had to have an "eye."

And she'd explain what the different kinds of seeds and plants were, why they were planted differently, how they would grow.

As spring changed to summer, the seeds and plants germinated and grew. The plot became a lush "garden of Eden" of maturing vegetables, and a great source of pride to her.

That was fifty years ago, and I have kept the education she gave me and used it many times since. I was the pupil; she was the teacher.

Newman's Woods

Newman's woods laid for a quarter-mile along the gravel town road I walked each day to my two-room country grade school. The woods stood as an island in a sea of farm fields.

Each morning I'd meet the neighbor kids from the north as they passed our farm driveway. And as we walked toward the old school, other youngsters would join us until a dozen of us of all ages and sizes would be gathered, ready for the day with Miss Ridge and Miss Lytle, our teachers.

School buses didn't exist back in those 1930 times. Country kids expected to walk, and walk we did. Our daily journeys, carrying our lard and tobacco pail lunch buckets, were marked by garter snake teasings of the girls, big guys picking on little guys and snowball fights.

For me, the deep woods along our route, with its brush-covered roadside, posed a foreboding sight.

During my early grade years, I feared to enter its bowels. But, by the time I reached nine or ten, and in the company of older, bolder classmates, I crossed that fear threshold and began to explore its dark innards.

And as the years passed, the woods became my personal sanctuary, my retreat, my wilderness.

By the time I reached my upper grades, very few days passed, when on my afternoon trips home, I didn't include a long, circuitous route through its oaks and hickories.

The woods became my private outdoor laboratory where, untaught, I learned. A world away from the world; a place where I touched, watched, listened and smelled the wonders of Mother Nature. Nothing perhaps, short of my birth, had a more lasting impact on my life.

Come autumn, and I knew where the biggest, cream-colored, fully-meated hickory nuts laid amidst their yellow-green husks beneath the shag-barked hickories. My Eight Brothers tobacco lunchpail would be filled to overflowing each night.

When the snows of winter blanketed my woods, there I learned the footprints of fox squirrels and cottontail rabbits. In the gathering dusk of the shortened days, I paused to listen in awe to the lonely, eerie hootings of the owls.

But springtime was the best.

As the days warmed, my woods began to stir. The little spring-fed stream, that curled its way through the meadow, came to life. And I'd lie on my belly on its bank and watch the crayfish scurry from rock to rock, their undertails laden with newly-hatching young.

The small pond, hidden amongst the trees, would echo to the voices of spring peepers. And I tiptoed across the marshy hummocks to dip a pint Mason jar into its cold water for a sample of slimey, stringy, black-beaded frog's eggs.

The forest floor would burst into a panorama of spring flowers. Dog-toothed violets, trilliums; blue, white and yellow violets. On the sunny south slopes, the golden buttercups grew in such profusion that I was hesitant to walk, the guilt of trampling their blooms so heavy.

A steady procession of birds returning from their migration flitted amongst the bushes and branches. Robins, juncos, bluebirds, warblers, grackles, mourning doves.

Nesting killdeers flushed before my feet, putting on their

broken-wing acts to lead me away from their young. Black hen crows sat fan-tailed on their nests of sticks high in the oak tops.

"Where have you been?" my mother would ask as I'd arrive late for supper, mud-stained, wet to the knees.

"In Newman's woods," I'd tell her. And somehow she understood.

I went back to Newman's woods awhile ago. It's gone now. Oh, a lot of trees are still there. But the woods is gone.

A woods is more than trees, you see.

In one corner a modernistic, many-windowed church has been built into a hillside. And under the oaks and hickories, palatial ranch-style homes with neatly manicured lawns now stand.

The little creek has been dammed, its free spirit stilled by an impassive gray concrete wall. Traffic zips along the old gravel road, now black-top, at forty miles an hour.

My old wilderness has disappeared, carried away by an insatiable something called progress.

And, yet, I know that I carried away the best part of it; its secrets, its wonders, its mysteries and the feelings it gave me those fifty years ago.

Every boy needs a woods. I know that now.

Tall Tales

He was a logger, I was a forester. He was getting up in years, I was young. He was a Menominee Indian, I was a white. He lived on the reservation, I lived on the outside. He was my friend, I was his friend.

His name was Lester Dickie. Everyone called him "Bogue". And I knew him back in the early 60's, back when I was the state's forester on the Menominee Indian Reservation, back in the days when the tribe was struggling with "termination" from federal supervision.

The Menominees own one of the finest forests in North America; white pine, hemlock, sugar maple, yellow birch four feet through and a hundred feet tall. A forest that has fed logs to their sawmill at Neopit since the turn-of-the-century.

Termination had placed the responsibility for the forest squarely on the shoulders of the state. I was the point man. "You are our eye in the sky," Alex Waupoose, the old logging superintendent, used to tell me.

Day-in and day-out, I worked with the Menominee people and I got to know them well, the loggers and woods workers especially. Most I knew on a first-name basis.

And that's how I got to know Bogue. I'd get around to each of the logging jobs every couple weeks. Bogue would be looking for me. He'd take a time-out, and we'd sit down on a big log and have a good visit.

He'd been a logger all of his life, and he'd tell me stories about the old days. Back when he rode the river drives down the Wolf and the Oconto. About the log jams; how dangerous they were to break. About the narrow gauge railroad logging days before the truck came to the woods. About the old-time camps with a hundred men or more.

As our friendship grew, so did the bond between us. And so began our tall-tale contest. Paul Bunyan-like stories; tales born in the minds of men who spend a lot of time alone, in the outdoors, with their thoughts.

First it would be his turn to tell one; then, the next trip, it would be mine. We'd sit there straight-faced and nod in false belief to each other as the latest figments of our imaginations were told.

Like the one Bogue told me about the time he was standing on the shore of a lake on the reservation. He saw what he thought was an island in the lake. But the island kept moving.

Perplexed, he got his canoe and paddled out to the "island." What he found, he said, was a huge old snapping turtle with trees and bushes growing on its back, swimming around in the lake.

Then there was the time I went muskie fishing up in the Park Falls country. "Bogue," I said, on my return, "The muskies are so big up there that they're mating with the deer when the deer come down to the lake to drink."

"Is that so?" he said, not cracking a smile.

"Yes," I replied. "I caught a 12-point muskie!"

"What did you do with it?" he asked.

"Well," I said, "I had to throw it back. The deer season's not open, you know."

And so it went.

Then, in 1966, came the day when I would leave the Menominees, promoted to a new job at Spooner. But

Bogue and I kept in touch. Letters now and then; cards at Christmas, wishing each other well.

Then, in 1970, the last letter from my old friend came. In a short while, he'd be gone. It's a special letter, from a special man. In it, he thanked me for writing, joshed me about an old experience, and said he was writing some "tales of the whispering pines."

But then, there was the P.S., and this is what it said:

"One time logging way back in the woods about twenty-five miles, we had a camp. We had an old Ford car to travel back and forth with our supply order to the train. I looked out toward the old car. I noticed one tire was all chewed up, them days all solid rubber. I had no spare, so I went to the cook camp and asked the cook to make a donut that size. He did, I used that the rest of the winter."

You topped me with that one, Bogue. You sure did.

A Powerful Lady

They're not big books, not filled with big words. And they're written by a lady who isn't much more than a tad over five feet tall. But they're big in what they say; big as life itself.

I'm talking about Esther Gibbs' two books, *"We Went A-Loggin' "* and *"This, That, and Tuther."*

I got to know Mrs. Gibbs only recently. A mutual friend had told me about her; that she lived only five miles from me; that she was eighty-two years old; that she'd gone on a hot air balloon ride to celebrate that last birthday.

Oh, I knew of her. Her first book had been on my shelf for better than ten years. But I wanted to meet this interesting person face-to-face. So I gave her a call. "Sure," she said, "Come on out and we'll visit."

A cold, windy snowstorm was blowing as I pulled into her driveway. But before I was out of the pickup, there she was on her back porch to greet me; no coat, no cap.

"You're going to catch yourself a good cold!" I called laughingly to her.

"I never catch a cold!" she came back; and as I've gotton to know her, I believe what she said. A cold germ woundn't stand a chance up against this sprite, feisty lady.

She invited me into the snug log cabin where she and her husband Cecil live; in through her kitchen where she still bakes bread on her Monarch wood-burning range, a stove like the one I carried wood to for a grandmother a long, long time ago.

And we talked. Talked about her writing, about her two books, about experiences she still wants to put on paper. And I picked up a copy of *"This, That, and Tuther"*, published only three years ago.

Well, I've read that book twice and her first book once again. They're my kind of books. Stories that tell it like it was forty, fifty, sixty years ago. Books written in plain talk by people who've been through the mill, seen it all. Stories that stir old memories, stories that I identify with.

I've always had a fascination with the history of northern Wisconsin. How the country was opened up, how the virgin timber was cut, how the backwoods farmer came with his plow to follow the axe. Over the years I've picked up a number of books that tell those stories.

And over those same years I've poked my way back into a lot of far corners of the cutover; back to long-abandoned homesteads where I've stood and pondered the lives that were lived there, the dreams that never came true.

Back to the remains of old logging camps where my boots kicked rusty axeheads and horseshoes, where, if I listened carefully, I hoped to hear the crash of a giant white pine coming down or the "whoa" of a teamster as he brought a turn of logs to a skidway.

And this lady has put some of this history down on paper. Not only what happened, but more importantly, how it felt. How it felt to be a young wife with a newborn son coping through the harsh winter back on an unplowed "spur" road while her husband was away in a logging camp, working to make a few bucks so they could afford to plant their stony fields come spring.

How she slept with an Army Colt 45 under her pillow and how she let a couple of no-goods know first-hand what the business end of it looked like. How one night she shot through the door at an intruder. Convinced she'd killed a man, she refused to look until the next day when her husband arrived and together in the entryway they found Porky, her pet pig that had broken out during the night, dead.

Her accounts of how she'd begged a logging camp boss for a job as camp cook are beautiful; a job she desperately wanted so that her young son could have the $150.00 hernia operation he needed. How it was to feed sixty-five men three times a day, seven days a week for an entire winter. What it took to daily cook a half a hog, a bushel of potatoes and twenty-five pounds of beans; not to mention baking twenty pies and a bushel of cookies, and more. All over a huge wood-burning stove with a day that began at five o'clock in the morning.

She tells about neighbors and friends that cared and shared. About the bad times and the good; about death and about laughter. For me, her stories are the heartbeat of this country back in those long-gone days.

They're powerful stories, powerfully written. But then, Esther Gibbs is a powerful lady.

Three Buildings

An ancient country church, an old farm house, an aged barn. Three structures that put a lot of mortar into the foundation of my life.

A few weeks ago I went back, back to my roots. Back to where I'd prayed, played and pondered as a boy.

The trip began last March actually. The telephone call came. I'd lost one of my favorite uncles. He was 86, and my godfather. The man that took me on my first fishing trips.

But I was fresh out of a hospital bed. I called, explained why I couldn't come to the funeral. Yet the pangs of guilt remained.

Then there was a second reason for going back, my mother. She's eighty now. I don't see her too often.

So Momma and I made the trip.

I called ahead, told my mother we were coming. And, as always, there she was waiting at the front door as the car pulled into the driveway. We visited, passed along the news from up north. And a plan was made. The next day we'd spend together. We'd go back to the farm that's been in the family for well over a hundred years; to her home country.

I drove the twelve miles out to the little country hamlet and parked beside the old yellow-brick church. 1883, its cornerstone reads. And slowly we walked into the cemetery, past the array of tombstones that go back to the 1850's. A predominantly German settlement, names like Eppers, Zeihen and Ludwig. And at the new grave I paid my respects.

"Would you like to go inside the church?" my mother asked.

"Yes, I would," I answered. Almost fifty years had passed since I'd been there.

"That's where I used to sing when I was a little girl," she said pointing to the choir loft. Then the altar. "There's where I got married," her voice gently echoing in the stillness.

Silently I gazed at the massive stained glass windows. The incredible beauty of the sunshine sifting through the colored glass; winged angels, bearded saints. And there, imprinted on the window he'd given when the church was built, was my great-grandfather's name.

I ran my hand over the backs of the red oak pews, their wood worn smooth by hard-working, honest farm people. Men with faces sun-browned from field toil. Sun-bonnetted ladies wearing high-button shoes, hushing restless youngsters.

Then the short drive to the old homestead. Built of red brick, the house was a mansion in its day. "Erected 1912" the white cornerstone states. Still standing true today on its hand-hewn granite block foundation, my grandfather had built it to last. Complete with indoor plumbing and old-fashioned gaslights, unheard of in its day; twelve rooms it had.

There, my grandfather raised his six sons and three daughters. Matt Kemen was his name. A man's name. And a man-and-a-half he was. *"The Boss"* his offspring always called him.

Around the old house I walked, letting old memories

flow. On the roof, the lightning rods still stand. Yet, out of place and incongruous in their midst, is a television antenna; the concession to inevitable change. On the long wood-pillared porch, where noon dinners were served on hot summer days, I stood.

Then on to the huge freshly-painted old barn. I wanted to be inside it one more time. Past where the tall windmill pumped its water before electricity came along. Past the milk house where, nightly, I turned the crank of the cream separator.

Through the door I slipped into the semi-darkness, to the musty smells of manure and hay and cattle, now gone. And there on a rough, unpainted board on the side of a calf-pen, I found one of the first marks I left for the world. Carved with my jackknife 47 years ago, *"RB July 1941"* it reads.

Past the horse stalls where Bobby and Billy, a team of grays my grandfather raised from colts and named after me and my brother, used to be tied. On to the cowbarn where I once sat on three-legged stools and stripped milk from Holsteins and Guernseys. I paused to touch the dusty wooden stanchions made from planks of oak and hickory cut from the farm's woodlot. Then on to the sheep shed where I helped my uncles dock the tails of new-born lambs.

And there, I finally, reluctantly turned and retraced my steps. I'd gone back. For a brief few hours, I'd re-lived my boyhood, savored its cherished memories. I'd found; I'd seen; I'd smelled; I'd touched my roots.

I found them, still there, in three old buildings.

A Valentine Verse

Valentine's Day in my old country school, a special time. Young love, puppy love; call it what you will. Kids growing up, getting in touch with their feelings; normal kids, doing normal things.

Somewhere around the sixth grade, the change began, as I recall. Until then, the boys hung around together; rassling, shooting marbles, building snow forts. And the same for the girls; skipping rope and playing jacks.

But at about eleven or twelve, a strange new chemistry entered our lives. Boys would find themselves compelled to hang by their knees from the chinning bar or stand on their heads for entire recesses. And the girls, theretofore content to clap erasers for the teacher, now gathered in little knots to whisper and giggle.

Not only did they act differently, they looked different. The little blonde in the seventh grade who had always played a mean second base, no longer looked like a second baseman. Her smile, the light in her eyes, no longer fit with baseball.

Little announcements written in white chalk on the sidewalk said things like "John + Mary." And carelessly passed notes on tablet paper would be confiscated by our teacher.

But come Valentine's Day and all those restless emotions could be given free rein.

A couple of the older girls would get the job of decorating a cardboard box with red and white crepe paper. And into a slit in the top, we slipped our penny-a-piece cupids and hearts. Some were pure courtesies, sent without envelopes. But there were always one or two special messages, carefully sealed, so secret that no eyes but the receiver were to see.

On the afternoon of the big day, our teacher would call a time out from classwork, and the big box would be opened. Names would be called and one-by-one the valentines handed out. It wasn't hard to see who the most popular girl or boy was. Some young dreams came true, some young hearts were broken — at least for a day or two.

A poem I read recently brought those wonderful days back.

Elgie McDonough is the author. He's a remarkable man. A retired farmer now seventy-seven years old; he and Iona, his wife of fifty years, live in Barron. He writes with rare sensitivity and recently published some of his works in a book, *"Poems 'N' Stuff."*

His Valentine Poem is the most touching love story I've ever read. With his permission, here is:

The Bashful Boy

He gave one peek at her pretty cheek
　　As they hurried home from school;
He would like to kiss her pretty lip
　　But she would think him just a fool.

He had been entranced with the pretty girl with the
　　dancing curl, as long as he could remember.
It must have been way back in June. . .
　　Or was it in December?

"I like your ma and I like your pa,
　　And I like your little brother;
So I wondered if occasionally
　　We could spend some time together?"

Well anyway he was going to say
   That he loved her true and tender —
If he could say the words where no one heard,
   So he would not offend her.

Then he mustered the nerve to say the word
   As they came to the little stream —
"May I carry your books as we cross the brook,"
   It seemed like a life-long dream.

"But can't you see how silly that'd be,
   'Cause you just had your twelfth birthday
I don't want to seem mean, but I'm thirteen,"
   And she looked the other way.

"But that don't mean much, the age and such,"
   And his voice began to bubble. . .
"If I grew an inch or two, I'd be as tall as you,
   And we would make a handsome couple."

She blushed real red and then she said,
   "I trust you know what you are saying."
"Oh yes I do, I'm in love with you" —
   There was no need denying.

With a wistful look she gave him the books,
   As they strolled across the stream. . .
The bashful boy and the girl with the curls,
   Began to share their dreams.

— — — — — —

Valentines; little verses, big meanings! Words that make
the world go round.

School Picnics

The sing-song chant rang across the schoolyard of my old country school. "School's out! School's out! The teachers let the monkeys out!" the words echoed.

The last day of school! In the pockets of our blue denim overalls were report cards. Forget the grades. All that mattered was one word at the bottom that read "Promoted." The nine months of struggling with arithmetic and spelling were over. Ahead laid a summer of bullhead fishing and slingshot shooting.

Miss Lytle and Miss Ridge, the teachers in my two-room school had looks of mixed relief and satisfaction, as they faced us for our final dismissal. Not only had they drilled some knowledge into our heads, but they'd been our parents away from our parents.

Not only had they been our educators, they'd been our disciplinarians, our counselors, our healers. Get caught whispering and you knew how to spell the word "whisper" after you spent a noon hour writing "I will not whisper in class" a hundred times.

Get smacked in the face with an icy snowball during recess in the dead of winter, and there they were to inspect a puffed lip, to check for loose teeth.

Today, I can understand those satisfied smiles. They'd done their jobs, and they'd done them well. And yet, as I look back, I can see more. I can see a touch of regret as we parted. Those old-time teachers were close to their kids. Parting was a bittersweet experience.

But one big day remained, the school picnic. Our final celebration. You don't hear much about school picnics any more. Perhaps they've gone the way of country schools.

The school picnic was our last hurrah for the school year. A chance for mothers and teachers to get together, relax, and talk about how we little darlings had done. We, at least us boys, really didn't care. We had other things on our minds. Forget school.

Back those fifty years ago, our picnics were held at a county park. The park was a nice place with lots of woods, the usual rustic tables, a well, and a baseball diamond.

But best of all, it had a river. Rivers had water in them, and water attracted me and my buddies like iron to a magnet. Sure, there'd be heaps of homemade bread sandwiches and lemonade-filled stone crocks with chunks of ice and halves of real lemons floating in them.

Sure, there'd be ribbons for the fifty-yard dash and the wheelbarrow and potato sack races. And maybe, just maybe, my gang would find a little time to compete.

But the river, that's what drew us. There you'd find us. Find us, that is, before and after the noon lunch.

The night before the big day, we'd dig ourselves a Prince Albert tobacco can of angleworms. Those old cans fit nice in a shirt pocket. And we'd inspect our fishing lines; throw lines, or "trow" lines as we called them. Lines wound on a chunk of wood, a small nut from the machine shed for a sinker, and the one fish hook we owned.

And the next day as soon as our feet touched the ground at the park, away we'd disappear. The older boys led the way. They knew the ropes. We younger squirts knew the peck order and kept our mouths shut, heeding the boisterous commands of the big guys.

Lines would be baited with wiggly worms, whirled in the air, and sailed out into the river. Fingers tensed, waiting for a bullhead or a sunfish to nibble. Maybe a sucker would pick up the bait. Suckers were big fish. Catch a sucker and you had yourself a trophy, a fish that brought looks of envy.

Get a snag and take off your shoes. Wade out, find the offending rock or submerged tree branch, and free the precious hook. Hooks were too valuable to lose.

And when the fish wouldn't bite, there was wading for crayfish, "crabs" we called them. Slowly lift a rock and with your other hand grab the critter as it tried to scoot backwards to safety.

Or catch clams. My idol, Lolo Godlewski, once told me he'd found a pearl in a clam. And whatever Lolo said, I believed. So feel the muddy bottom with barefeet, and with our trusty jackknives, open the shells to probe the creamy innards for that elusive pearl.

And when our stomachs announced it was noon, back we'd drift to the picnic tables. Wet, smelly, muddy, scratched; proudly carrying a bullhead or two on a crotched willow stick.

The prissy girls would wrinkle their noses in disgust. Mothers would exchange knowing, resigned sighs. "Boys will be boys," someone would offer.

School picnics, they sure were fun.

Real Bull in the Bullpen

All the hassling going on in the big leagues over tampered baseballs and bats brings back some good chuckles. Scuffed baseballs! Corked bats! Those umps should have been around my neighborhood when I was a youngster.

Back in those days there wasn't much for country kids to do in the summer but play baseball. Sure, we could dig ourselves a can of angleworms, grab our fish poles, and walk the four miles over to the river for some bullhead fishing. And we did.

But baseball was the big thing. If we weren't under orders to weed the garden, help shock oats, or something like that; we played baseball.

There wasn't always a full-fledged game. Lots of times we just played "catch", tossing a ball back and forth to each other; trying to figure out how to throw a curve.

Then there were the games of "500" where we hit flies and grounders to each other. Catch a grounder cleanly, and it was worth fifty points. Snag a fly without dropping it, and you got a hundred points. Add up your points, and when you reached five hundred, it was your turn to bat. Playing 500 had another advantage; it was good for your arithmetic.

But let's talk about balls and bats. A new ball was unknown. The best I could hope for was a fair used one from a benevolent baseball-playing uncle.

And we literally beat those balls to death. They'd take just so much pounding, and then the stitches would begin to break. When the cover started to hum going through the air, it was time for repairs.

It was then that I'd nose around my mother's sewing machine until I found a good-sized darning needle and some stout black linen thread. Painstakingly, I'd sew the cover back on the ball.

All the kids in the neighborhood knew how to sew a baseball. The art was handed down from the older kids to the younger ones.

Well, there were just so many repair jobs that you could do on a ball. Finally there'd be one line drive too many, and the cover would split like a half-peeled orange. Then it was time for the ultimate repair job.

Out to the machine shed I'd go and find a roll of friction tape. Not the fancy plastic stuff we have today. The old-fashioned kind with strings in it. And I'd rip the ragged cover off that good old ball and wrap the innards with several layers of black tape.

A taped ball was a dead ball. Hit it a good whack and it would kind of go "poof." But it was better than no ball at all.

Bats were the same story. Crack the handle on a hard inside fast ball and off I'd go to the machine shed again. Scrounge around for some shingle nails, hammer a couple into the handle and wind on some more of that good friction tape. There were very few bats in the neighborhood that hadn't been patched up at least once.

Then there were our baseball gloves, "mitts" we called them. First you had to be lucky to own one. Lots of kids played bare-handed.

I got my first mitt by saving ice cream bar wrappers. I'd

walk out to the county park and hang around the concession stand. When someone bought a nickel ice cream bar, I'd ask for the wrapper. I must have collected a thousand. But I sent them in, and in a couple weeks the mailman brought my catcher's mitt.

And our baseball diamonds? None of those neatly manicured fields with fancy bases for us. We played our games in a corner of the pasture where the cows kept the grass mowed.

On Sunday afternoons we'd gather for a real game. Kids came from all around; walking, or riding their skinny-tired bikes, carrying their nondescript bats, balls and mitts.

Adult supervision? Never heard of it. We'd choose up sides, and have at it.

Those were some games. Talk about doctored baseballs. Let a grounder to shortstop be hit where a cow had paused the day before, and it took a lot of intestinal fortitude to make the throw to first base.

Have a foul ball sail over into the cornfield and the game stopped while everyone looked for that precious sphere until it was found.

And action in the bullpen? We had a real bull in ours.

So I'm not the least bit impressed today with the rhubarb going on over sandpaper and emery boards.

Stuff like that would have been strictly minor league in my neck of the woods fifty years ago.

The Edgewood School

The old schoolhouse used to stand about a quarter mile down the gravel town road from my tree farm. "Edgewood," it was called.

An old map had told me where it once stood. Twenty years ago, I'd walked into the woods to locate the site; then long grown back to popples, oaks and hazelbrush.

Over the years, as I've passed, I've gazed into the thick forest. And feelings, memories of my own country-school days come back to me.

I can see country kids raucously racing around the schoolyard, boys wrestling, girls skipping rope. I can hear the ting-a-ling of a bell as a young teacher brings her charges back to their desks. I can taste homemade bread sandwiches lined with apple butter or fried eggs.

There was a time when the hinterlands of Wisconsin were dotted with one-room country schools. Look at the old maps and you can find them, spaced about four miles apart. In those long-gone days youngsters walked to school. Two miles seemed to be the standard for maximum distance.

But then came better roads, school buses, consolidations. Today, kids ride a bus for an hour to go to school in town. Country schools are a faded chapter in our educational history.

But I can't forget. And I couldn't put Edgewood out of

my mind.

Last fall, I'd again walked back to the crumbling foundation. I'd kicked the matted leaves and grass, hoping to uncover an old ink bottle, maybe an Indian head penny. I'd looked. I'd listened.

But all I came away with was an undeniable need to know the old school's story.

I found that story the other day.

My wife and I visited Hattie Lubben, a nearby neighbor. She's 88 years young now; lived all of those years a few miles north of Stone Lake. She's a true pioneer in our country.

I'd met Hattie before. Years ago, I'd bought some pine logs from her and her husband, Herman, to build my little cabin back in the popples. Herman passed away in 1971. But Hattie still lives in the snug farmhouse they built together back in 1920.

"Please tell me about the Edgewood school," I said to her. She did. And I thank her.

"The school was built in 1905," she told me. "It opened with five children. I started the first grade there in 1906."

Her father had helped build the school, she said. "He was always on the school board. And Herman, my husband, was on the board for many years. Both my children went there."

"What did it look like?" I asked.

"It was just a frame building, one room," she answered. "It was painted white on the outside and blue-gray on the inside. Out back there was a woodshed and two outdoor toilets, one for the boys, and other for the girls."

"What did it look like inside?" I continued.

"On one end there was a big box stove. The teacher built the fires. Of course, there was no electricity. The north and south walls were almost entirely windows. That was the light we studied by. There was a kerosene lamp, but that was only used for doings in the evenings.''

Sometimes there were only two or three children besides herself in the school. ''There was never more than 16 in the eight grades,'' she said.

How did the kids dress, I asked. ''We all wore long underwear and homeknit wool socks up to our knees, hightop shoes and four-buckle overshoes, in the winter. Girls wore long skirts down to their shoetops. Showing your ankles was considered daring,'' she replied with a smile.

''What did you do at recesses?'' I asked.

''We played hide-and-seek; a game called steal-a-crown; some of the boys played marbles. In winter, the boys built a snow slide down a hill. Some of the Norwegian kids had long homemade skis. They'd ski down that slide and end up in a heap at the bottom.''

''What did you study?''

''Reading, arithmetic, geography, spelling, penmanship. There weren't fountain pens in those days. We used quill pens and dipped them in ink wells in our desks,'' she told.

What did the countryside look like, I inquired.

''There was a lot more pine but much had been logged. Forest fires were terrible. Roads were just trails through the woods, built with hand tools and horses. In the winter they weren't plowed. Sometimes my brother took me to school with the team.''

And Christmas?

''The boys would get a nice spruce from a swamp. We had candles on it. Our Christmas programs were always in the afternoon. We used to put on pretty nice programs, even plays.''

She told me the names of her teachers, how the coyotes howled at night, how sweet the wild arbutus flowers smelled. And much more. Wonderful words from a wonderful lady.

And now, the old Edgewood school has new meaning to me. As I pass, I see it with new eyes, vision that cuts through 83 years of the past.

A nice lady, Hattie Lubben, gave me those eyes.

A Trip Up North

Right about now, people down south are thinking about coming up north — to vacation, to relax.

Up North! As a youngster, what a thrill it was to hear those words. Up North was a mystical, magical place; a camelot far over the horizon. A place that conjured visions of mammoth fish waiting to be caught, of sixteen point bucks hiding behind every tree.

Those were 1930 times, and I was growing up in southern Wisconsin. And I lived to hunt and fish. Sure we had game around. Sure we had fish. But every hunter and fisherman dreams of greener pastures, faraway places where the catch can exceed even the wildest expectations.

Such was Up North.

When an uncle of mine would announce that he was headed "up north" to do some fishing, I listened with bated breath as he talked about his pending adventure. And I darned near died of excitement as I waited for him to return, to listen to his tales of big northerns that smacked his Heddon River Runts.

Times then were different; the cars, the highways, the leisure time. A week's vacation was a big deal. A neighbor or two even suggested that anyone wasting valuable time and money to travel the horrendous distance of 300 miles to go fishing just didn't have his head on straight. Neighbors like that, I figured, we didn't need. And I viewed them with suspicion forever after.

A trip up north was a major expedition. Two days one way, the journey would take. Letters would go out to "distant" relatives upstate, and arrangements made for an overnight stay. A chance for a short visit, and the price of a hotel room saved.

The night before departure was a frenzy of activity as the Pontiacs and Chevies of the era, cars with yellow wooden-spoked wheels and gear shift levers by the front seat, were loaded.

In would go a battered black suitcase packed with freshly-washed work clothes. Then an old metal tackle box holding spare fishhooks, sinkers and cork bobbers. Maybe there'd be a new Daredevil or Bassoreno plug, last minute splurges of a couple hard-earned bucks. And into a safe niche in the back seat, a steel bait casting rod, with a Pflueger reel attached, would be tucked.

In the coolest corner of the car would be stowed a pail of moist garden dirt. The pail would hold a week's supply of night crawlers, if they survived the trip, that is.

And last, the bamboo cane poles, sixteen-footers wrapped in a gunny sack and tied to the roof of the car. Cars in those days had radiator caps and trunk handles, things you could tie things to.

A fitful night's sleep and up before dawn. A quick breakfast, a shoebox filled with sandwiches, and time to hit the road.

The old concrete highways were narrow and winding. Unlike today, they went through, not around towns. Yet those old roads were fun to travel. The pace was leisurely; past one-pump gas stations, by strings of Burma Shave signs with their catchy little jingles.

Through towns with unfamiliar names, towns from the other side of the world for me. Wausau, Phillips,

Woodruff, Manitowish! Places up north.

The second day we'd find, at the end of a tree-lined sand trail, a little cabin waiting. Nothing fancy, just two rooms; one for cooking and eating, the other for sleeping.

Handshakes would be exchanged with the resort proprietor and his wife, and questions asked about the fishing. Then a quick walk down to the dock to check out the wooden cedar-strip boat tied there. And an eye-feasting look at the lake.

The fishing fever would build.

The car would be unloaded, a grocery list made, and a drive into town to a small mom-and-pop store to stock up for the week.

Last, and best of all, there'd be a stop at the local live bait shop. More fishing talk, and into an old-fashioned minnow pail, the kind with a steel flap on top, would go a good ration of mud minnows. Mud minnows were tough. They stayed alive. You don't see mud minnows sold any more. That's too bad.

We'd arrived!

We were "up north" where the scent of pine trees freshens the air, where chipmunks play hide-and-seek amongst the white birch, and red squirrels chatter overhead. Where the music of gentle waves splashing softly against a rocky shore lulls one to sleep at night.

Where vacations always end too soon.

Trout Fishing in Japan

Ever stop at a trout hatchery and look at the fish? There they swim, in a black swarm, hungrily begging for a morsel of food to be tossed. If you have, then you know the thought that crosses your mind, "Boy, would I like to throw a hook in there!"

I had the privilege of fishing in a trout hatchery once, back in 1946, in Japan. And it was all perfectly legal and legitimate.

Back then, I was a GI pulling occupation duty, a weatherman with the Fifth Air Force. My job was to help run the weather station at the Atsugi Air Base a few miles outside Tokyo.

The station was General Douglas Mac Arthur's home base, and I had the opportunity to see the old gentleman of "I shall return" fame several times when he came out to greet visiting dignitaries.

In comparison to a lot of military assignments, my job was a good one. Though I'd have preferred to be back home getting on with more important things in my life, I couldn't complain. My work was interesting, as we gathered weather information 24 hours a day from all over the western Pacific and eastern Asia. I liked my job.

The dozen or so of us in our little group had reasonably decent quarters, the food was good, as far as mess hall food went, and we had the freedom to come and go on our time off.

But there was something I missed, and missed badly, a chance to go fishing. Man, how I yearned to go fishing.

There was water around, rivers and the ocean. And a time or two I watched Japanese men cast their nets to catch a few sardine-size fish. But that didn't count, that didn't look like real fishing.

My best buddy, Ed, liked to fish too. And we'd talk about fishing. Somehow, we just had to figure out a way to go.

Well, as fate would have it, we'd got to know a couple of Japanese nationals, two brothers who spoke English fluently. About our age, they'd lived for a time in the United States before the war broke out. And as our acquaintanceship grew, Ed and I mentioned how badly we wanted to go fishing.

Fishing? They'd take us fishing, they said. They knew a place. But it was a long drive back into the mountains, in the interior of the country. A man they knew owned a trout hatchery there, a man that manufactured cameras.

Cameras, shameras! Ed and I didn't care. Let's go, we said. And the trip was arranged.

Now, the captain in charge of our unit was a good guy. Ed and I explained to him that we wanted to borrow the four-wheel-drive Dodge power wagon over the weekend. I think he knew something was fishy, but he didn't say no. And on a Friday night we packed up, picked up our two Japanese guides, and headed out.

Talk about a trip! All night we drove, over some of the worst roads I've ever been on in my life; narrow, twisting trails that clung to the mountainsides, where I could look straight down a thousand feet in the moonlight.

Our Japanese friends had never been back in there before either, and their map wasn't much. But we only got lost once. And come daybreak, we arrived; exhausted, half-dead from no sleep.

But there in front of us, shimmering in the dawn's first light, laid the trout ponds; a beautiful sight with real fish, rainbow trout dimpling the water as they rose to snatch low-flying insects.

And there stood our host, the Japanese cameraman, smiling graciously to greet us. Nearby, standing quietly, was a handful of young Japanese boys, anxious to watch the American soldiers catch fish.

Our host handed us two of those old-fashioned telescopic steel fly rods rigged with hook and line. For bait, we'd use silkworm larvae. And it didn't take Ed and me long to get into action.

As fast as we'd cast a bait into the water, a trout would nail it, fish that ran about fifteen inches. It was like — well, like fishing in a trout hatchery.

We didn't take too many, maybe thirty or so. And then, the Japanese boys cleaned our fish, packing them in ice in the ammunition compartment of the Dodge for our trip home.

On the premises, our host had a little cottage, to which he invited us. There we relaxed the rest of the day. That night he joined us for supper, and the next day we retraced the tortuous mountain trails back to Atsugi.

We'd gone fishing. And lord, it had felt good.

Travelling by Thumb

The snowstorm travel problems over the holidays reminded me of my old hitch-hiking days.

For about five years in the late 40's, while I was in the Army Air Force and college, I travelled mainly by my thumb.

Being a buck private in the service in 1945, I wasn't exactly what you'd call affluent. Pulling the tidy sum of $21.00 a month meant that I had to watch my budget more than close. Buses and trains cost money. Planes were out of the question.

So I did what a lot of GI's did; I travelled by thumb.

Now, being in uniform back in those days had a lot of advantages. The sneak attack by the Japanese on Pearl Harbor had galvanized the nation. No doubt existed about what had to be done. Win the war. And anyone that represented a part of the fight was treated with respect by the civilian populace. People were happy to help a serviceman.

So, out to the gate of the Chanute Field Air Base at Rantoul, Illinois I'd walk, show my Christmas pass to the MP, and step onto the shoulder of US 45. My thumb would only have to be in the air for a half dozen cars or so, and I'd be on my way north toward Wisconsin.

The interstate highways didn't exist in those days. Even the best roads went through cities, not around. Once in awhile I'd get lucky and hitch a ride with someone going a long distance. But most were short hops from one small burg to the next.

Looking back, considering the stresses of those war years, hitch-hiking was a rewarding experience. True, I met a few weirdos, both men and women. But most of the people I rode with were fine folks. They'd ask questions about my service activities, where I was going; why.

And when the point arrived where we'd part, there were sincere best wishes and regrets that they couldn't take me further. Like two ships passing in the night, for a brief time we'd got to know each other a bit. Then the car door would open and I'd leave. Never again would we meet.

Out I'd step, stick my thumb in the air, and the whole process would start all over.

I covered a lot of miles hitch-hiking. And I met a lot of nice people. Many were the times when I had folks insist on paying for my meal when we stopped to eat. Many times I had people go out of their way to drop me off at a good spot to catch a ride. Once I had a kind old gentleman drive some twenty miles out of his way to take me right to the door of my home.

But the most memorable hitch-hiking experience I ever had happened over the holidays in 1945.

I'd hitch-hiked home from Chanute Field for a visit. Yet in my brain was an invitation from a young lady and her family in Ohio. I'd met her before I'd been called into service while I was playing baseball in the Ohio State League. Come and visit us over the holidays, she'd written.

So after a few days at home, I packed up my barracks bag and headed south and east — by thumb.

Well, I made it. And after a couple days of socializing, the time came to head back to the base. And west my thumb and I headed, on old US 40.

Now, on my route laid Indianapolis, a big town. I didn't want to hitch-hike through Indianapolis. So I checked my map and found a little state highway that swung around the city. Along the road laid three tiny cross-road hamlets. No problem.

Well, I got off of US 40 at the intersection, and proceeded to hook a ride. The driver said he could only take me to the first little burg. OK. When we arrived there, out of the car I got.

The traffic on the little road wasn't all that much. There I stood, waiting as night came on. Then here comes an old Model "A" Ford with an elderly gent behind the wheel, looking me over suspiciously. And he passes me by.

Well, in a couple minutes, along comes another car that picks me up. Going only to the next town, the driver says. Down the road we move, and shortly we pass the old Model A. And when we get to the second town, out I get.

There I am, standing on the shoulder, and pretty soon here comes the Ford. Well, the old gent sees me and gets a surprised look on his face. But again he doesn't stop.

Well, the same thing happens. Another car, one that picks me up. A few miles and we pass the Model A. And at the third little town, I get dropped off.

I'm standing there, and once more here comes the old codger. By this time I'm smiling over the whole thing as he slowly approaches. He takes one look, hits the brakes, and almost stands that old Ford on her radiator. And he takes me right out to US 40 west of Indianapolis.

He was a nice old fellow.

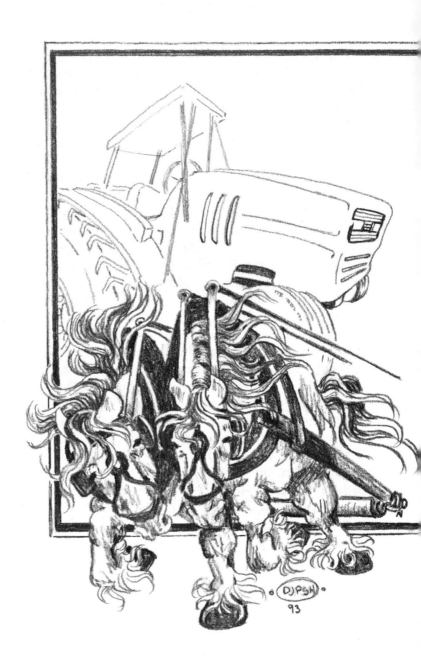

Horsepower

Farming with horses. You don't see many horses around the countryside anymore. And those that you do see, are riding horses, the kind you find in parades and rodeos.

There was a time when horses were big on farms; the mainstay source of power. A farmer was judged by how many "teams" he owned.

I grew up around horses. Horsebarns were a standard fixture on my two grandfathers' farms and my father's. Feeding, watering and "cleaning out the barn" were daily chores, and I got very familiar with the handles of hay forks and manure forks.

Oh sure, we had tractors around. The popular model in our neighborhood was the 10-20 McCormick Deering. They were squat, powerful machines, built for slow, heavy pulling. Made with solid steel wheels that had four-inch pointed cleats, I always figured they were the forerunner of the Army's tanks that General Patton used to kick Hitler's butt back in World War II.

Our tractors were usually reserved for pulling the long belts that turned the pullies on the thrashing machine and silo filler. Our horses were used where speed and mobility were needed; duties like pulling hay mowers, grain wagons and corn cultivators.

Both my grandfathers were good horsemen. They knew horses. The old saying about never looking a gift horse in the mouth is true. I watched my grandfathers check the teeth on many a horse to verify its age and condition.

And they raised horses. There was always a colt or two down in the pasture, a product of one of their mares. Replacement animals for Jim, Dan or Maude when they couldn't do the job any more.

In fact, one of my grandfathers raised a pair of "grays" that he called Bobby and Billy, the names of his first two grandchildren, me and my brother.

So I've got a warm spot in my heart for those big, plodding, most-of-the-time gentle beasts.

Back in the 1930's, if you were born on a farm, it was only natural to assume that you'd stay on the farm. That was the way it had always been. And part of all that meant learning to care for and handle horses.

How many people today could harness a team of horses and hitch them to a hay wagon? Not too many I expect. But I'd learned to do it by the time I was twelve years old. Sure I'd have to stand on my tiptoes to slip the bridle over the horse's ears, to put the bit in its mouth, to snap some of the buckles on the harness. And I'd have to watch my barefeet. A sudden unexpected move by one of those big hooves would mean a pinched big toe.

But there was a feeling of power and authority when they were finally ready; and with a slap of the "lines" on their rumps and a "giddap," you'd move them forward, their long tails switching; an eagerness in their gait, as they began their day's work.

Putting up hay was a big time for horses. Making hay was different then; no balers, no chopping, no haylage for the silo.

Haying began with a team of horses hitched to a two-wheeled mower with a long sickle bar. I'd watch, fascinated, as my grandfather made the rounds of a field of timothy, alfalfa, clover; laying down the swaths. The corners of the field were the most interesting. There's where I'd hear the, "Whoa! Back up Jim, Dan! Now giddap!" as he made the turn.

Next would come the raking with the side-delivery rake to roll the hay into long windrows.

And finally came the horses and wagon with the old-fashioned hay loader towed behind. One of the first real jobs I had was driving horses on a hay wagon. I'd stand there under my straw hat, my bare toes hooked on a rung of the ladder up front, and with the two leather strap lines guide the team along the windrows.

I haven't seen a farm boy driving a team of horses for years. Maybe it's for the better. Maybe it's more fun today to drive a big green-and-yellow, rubber-tired, air-conditioned tractor with a chopper running off the power take-off.

Maybe it's more fun to turn a key and have a hundred horsepower diesel jump to life; horsepower that you don't have to let take a "blow" in the shade of a chokecherry tree along a fenceline.

Maybe it is, but then I wouldn't know.

Thrashing Time

My folks always called it "thrashing" time. But my teacher in our little country school called it "threshing." The first few times she called it that I didn't know what she was talking about.

Maybe she didn't know as much about our country ways as she should have. Or on the other hand, perhaps she felt it wise to set us country bumpkins straight with our vocabulary.

Nevertheless, around the neighborhood farms that mid-summer period when the oats, barley and wheat were ready for harvest was always called thrashing. And thrashing time was the biggest social event of the year. The only thing that came close was the annual Sunday church picnic. Or a "shivaree" for a long-time bachelor that suddenly decided to take a wife.

Times were tough on the farm fifty years ago. People pulled together, helped each other out. And so a dozen farmers around our place had banded together and bought a thrashing machine. Individually they couldn't afford to own one. Collectively they could.

Early August found the machine being moved from neighbor to neighbor, pausing at each farm for a few days until the precious grain was safely stored in bins for the winter.

My grandfather was the leader of the group. The

Machine Man, they called him. His job was to oversee the operation. To make sure the big Case separator, with its name and an eagle's head emblazoned in brilliant red and gold on its side, was properly positioned; its belts securely tightened; its grease cups always filled.

Gramp was also the man catcher. Extra help was needed; hands to pitch the bundles of grain, to carry the canvas bags into graneries, to stack the straw.

Gramp was good at finding men. Off to town he'd go and hit a couple back alley saloons. And the next day, strong-backed, heavy-muscled men, willing to work for a couple dollars a day and a square meal, would show up. Finding men willing to work in those Depression-day times was no problem.

Thrashing gave me my first real job. Oh, I'd earned a few nickels around home. But that didn't count. A real job was when you worked for someone else.

Gramp hired me; I'd be his "blower man." I suppose I was about twelve. My job would be to run the blower on the machine, the long sheet metal tube through which the grain straw was vented. Fifty cents a day I'd receive from the farmer.

Now, being the blower man was no small responsibility. Each morning I'd climb up to the top of the big separator; and there, amidst churning belts, whirling pullies, and clouds of swirling grain chaff, I'd sit.

In front of me were the worm gear controls to move the blower horizontally or raise it vertically. Along the top were the ropes which I pulled to open and close the hinged snout. The straw spouted in a steady stream from the blower. Spread the straw evenly into a neat stack; that was my job.

Come noon, the crew would break for dinner. What a heady feeling it was for a young kid to stand in line for a turn at the wash basins setting on benches out on the lawn, surrounded by maybe twenty grown men.

And when the call came that the meal was waiting, in I'd march with them to the long tables loaded with food. There I'd sit next to Grandpa, listening to menfolk talk, proud as a peacock to be part of the grown-up world.

All the while, a half-dozen ladies would be scurrying about, their faces beet-red from working over wood-burning cook stoves all morning. The meal had to be a good one. People were known to talk. And no self-respecting farm wife wanted the reputation of being a questionable cook.

So the heaping platters and bowls of mashed potatoes, baked ham, roast beef, fresh peas from the garden, and the ripest, plumpest tomatoes had to be just right. The apple and cherry pies had to have crusts so tender they'd almost melt in your mouth.

A few days later when the thrashing was done, the farmer would pay the crew. From man to man he'd move, counting out dollar bills and fifty cent pieces. Usually I was the last to be "settled up with."

But it made no matter. When a Lichter or a Heimes or a Sinnen reached into the front pocket of his faded blue bib overalls, took out his battered black leather pocketbook and handed me my dollar-and-a-half, I stood ten feet tall inside.

"See you next year," he'd say and I knew he meant it.

I'd had a real job! I'd been a blower MAN!

Fourth of July

I'm glad to see the Fourth of July toned down.

Back in my boyhood days, my buddies and I carried enough gunpowder around in the pockets of our bib overalls to blow ourselves to kingdom come, were the stuff to go off.

One hears today that parents are more liberal with their kids. Not true in my book. I shudder when I think about the week of the Fourth in those old days. Later in life, I sure didn't let my kids pull the stuff I did. And I'd die a thousand deaths if I thought my grandchildren were.

Back in those late 30's, the Fourth was a big deal, a time that we looked forward to with great excitement. And the biggest part of the deal was the anticipation of shooting fireworks. For weeks, I'd save my nickels and dimes so I'd have a couple bucks to blow in, or better, blow up. "Fourth of July money" we called it.

A week or two ahead of the big day, little stands slapped together with odds and ends of lumber would pop up around the country. Along the main roads and in every little hamlet, brightly-painted banners announced fireworks for sale.

The stands were hubbubs of activity, and noise. As Fourth fever built, people stopped to pick up their supplies. The boxes of firecrackers, cherry bombs, skyrockets and sparklers were a sight to see, fascinating in their brilliant cellophane wrappers with pictures of dragons and Chinese hieroglyphics on the labels.

And, of course, very few people could resist the temptation to try out their wares. Packages would be opened, fuses carefully untangled, and a few samples tested to make sure they worked and were loud enough.

My buddies and I were no different. We'd ride our bikes over to the nearest stand, carefully study the various sizes and brands, and finally lay our hard-earned money down. Home we'd go with our Fourth loot.

The weather for the big day always seemed to be the same, dawning sunny, hot and still. Still, that is, until breakfast time had passed. Then the country side would begin to echo to the sounds of exploding gunpowder.

Even the roads. It was common to see black Model A Fords moving down the gravel roads, windows rolled down, and a couple local sports sitting in the front seat tossing sizzling firecrackers out to explode in the ditches.

Mailboxes were favorite targets. Open the box, toss in a lighted three-incher, and take off. The day after the Fourth, most mailboxes had a layer of shredded red and blue paper in them.

Luckily, I developed a healthy fear of firecrackers early on. I never bought the real big jobs, mainly because they cost too much. But I didn't go for the half-inch "lady fingers" either, not enough punch.

But I got pretty good with the two-inchers, very innovative. Equipped with the stick of brown, slow-burning "punk" that the vendors always threw in free with my purchase, I'd find me a small tin can. Place the can on a good flat surface bottomside up, slip a cracker under it, and touch it off. I could send that can fifty feet in the air.

Some brave, or stupid, souls prided themselves on holding crackers in their fingers, lighting and tossing the missiles before they blew. I never got into that — too chicken.

I'll never forget one Fourth. I was standing in the driveway of my grandfather's farm, busy splintering a wood fence post with my firecrackers.

A young man who lived down the road had walked over for a visit with my uncles. Now here he comes down the lane, headed for home, all dressed up in his holiday white shirt, smoking half a cigar. As he approached, he saw what I was doing.

"Whatsa matter? You afraid to throw 'em?" the dude said to me.

Actually I was and meekly answered, "Well, the fuses burn kinda fast."

"Here, lemme show ya," he cockily said, reaching for a cracker. I handed him one.

Taking the cigar from his lips, the good old boy touched it to the cracker's fuse. Fssst! Pow! The little bomb exploded in his hand. I'll never forget the sight of him walking out the lane shaking his right hand trying to restore some feeling.

I have to honestly say that I never knew anyone back in those times that lost an eye or was seriously burned by fireworks. But that was only the luck of the draw. It happened, and too often.

I'm a hundred percent behind the controls we have today on fireworks. Life, after all, is a lot like a firecracker. Sometimes the fuse burns too fast.

An Old Baseball Bat

The old baseball bat stands in a corner next to my desk now. Made of brown-stained ash, my mother found it tucked away in a far cranny of an upstairs closet where I'd left it many years ago.

But it's more than an old baseball bat. It's a chronicle of a time when baseball was the biggest thing in a 13-year-old's life, when baseball was his all-consuming dream.

And it's a trophy, a treasured keepsake of a summer when a motley bunch of plain and simple country kids achieved something in their lives. For there, on its upper barrel end, etched in black letters charred with my burning glass 49 years ago, are the words "1940 CHAMPS."

Back when I was a boy, every kid owned a burning glass. A burning glass was nothing more than a magnifying glass. And for hours we'd sit focusing the sun's rays on a piece of wood, engraving designs and names.

I remember the day my father bought the old bat for me. We were in a store in town. While my dad went about his business, I wandered about, browsing. And there, in a wooden crate, stood the baseball bats.

One by one, I hefted them; savoring their smoothness, testing their weight, their balance. My hands told me that one was special, that one would surely hit home runs for me.

Apprehensively, I carried my prize over to my father. Would he buy it for me? The price tag said $1.35, a tidy sum for a farmer just beginning to bounce back from the Depression. My pleading eyes met his. For a moment he paused, silently studying my face. And then he reached into his worn black pocketbook and laid the money on the counter.

Today, the old bat shows the scars, the rigors of the baseball wars I put it through. It's handle is cracked, patched with shingle nails to keep it from splintering in two. Old fashioned black friction tape spirals up its handle to provide added strength and a better grip for my sweaty hands.

And at the butt are two notches carved with my jack knife long ago, to mark the home runs I'd lofted far over opposing left fielders' heads.

Next to the trademark, once more etched in big black bold letters, is the name of our school, "Hillcrest." For, from our recesses and noon hours, our baseball team had been born. The Hillcrest Hellraisers, we called ourselves.

Circling the fat end of the bat, neatly etched in the brown wood, are twelve names. First names like my own, and Bill, Jim, Nick and Joe.

We were a wild crew. Not in a bad sense. Just free-spirited country boys who fished, hunted, went to school together — and played baseball. And we were lean. Except for our first baseman, who was appropriately nicknamed "Fat," there wasn't an ounce of extra flesh on any of us. We could run like the wind.

The Hillcrest Hellraisers played that 1940 summer in the county recreation league. Once a week, we'd take on teams like Berryville, Bullamore Forks and Pike River. One by one, we knocked them off. And as summer closed, we'd finished in first place in our eastern division.

And, finally, we'd play New Munster, the winner of the western division, for the county championship. Best of all, we'd play at night under lights, heady stuff for a crew of country bumpkins.

I remember the series well. Two games of three we had to win. What a thrill it was to play before cheering crowds of partisan parents and relatives.

I was the catcher. There I'd squat, behind home plate, as our pitcher whistled fastballs past the swinging bats of the enemy hitters. And when the final out of the second game was made, we'd won. We were the champions of the county!

I look at the old bat today, and reminisce about my past teammates.

Two, our pitcher and third baseman, are long gone; their lives snuffed out by an oak tree when their car missed a curve. The left fielder, he spent six years in the Pacific in World War II. When he came home, people said he was different. The people that said that hadn't been to the Pacific.

The shortstop, he went on to be a high school teacher and baseball coach, taking his teams to state tournaments. And another outfielder, he became a successful lawyer.

And the catcher, today he just fondles the old bat and reads its story.

No Roads Here Then

"Right over there is where the tar paper shanty stood," Nels Olson said, pointing his finger toward the window. "And back there, where you see those popples and white birches, that was the potato patch."

I was sitting with Nels in the sun porch of his trim, red brick home on a lonely gravel road in the wild back country of Bayfield County a few miles west of Mason, a small country village that's seen a lot of change pass it by.

The house, the land it rests on, Nels and his wife, Frances; the countryside, even Mason itself, all represent a documentary; one of life in northern Wisconsin for almost a century.

I knew the story pretty well. I'd read it in a book I'd received, *"Time In Many Places,"* written by Nels. "I spent six years writing it," he told me. "I was 79 when I finished it." He's 87 now.

Amazing, I thought. But then Nels Olson is an amazing man. Still spry, though he's got some back ailments, he's sharp as a tack; wonderful to visit with.

The story begins on October 11, 1902 in a little town in Norway — Fevig, where Nels was born; one of four children. Two years later, his father emigrated to America, hoping to find "better opportunities than in Norway", coming to Mason where he found a job in the sawmill there on the White River. By 1906, he'd saved enough money to send for his family.

Not quite four, Nels remembers their departure from Norway on a steamer for America. "There was much weeping when our ship finally got under way," he writes. Passengers sang (in Norwegian), "I'm leaving for America and will never come back again."

And he describes the ocean trip, the thrill of seeing the Statue of Liberty, Ellis Island, the horse drawn carriages of New York, their arrival by train at Mason in June of 1906, and the reunion there with his "papa", a father he barely knew.

By horse and wagon, they travelled the last few miles; moving into the tar paper shanty his grandparents had built on a forty back in the woods. "There were no roads here then," Nels told me the other day. "Just logging trails."

Thus, Nels Olson began life in America, a life marked with struggle, sacrifice and incredible hardship; yet rich in love, family kinship, and his Lutheran faith.

And he's written eloquently about both sides of that life.

Today, for example, he resides on the same soil that he first called home those 84 years ago. He owns the forty acres that his grandparents, Nils and Aase Torgeson, homesteaded on.

He tells of the hard work he knew as a boy, of cutting trees and grubbing stumps to clear land for farming. Of hand-me-down clothes and running barefoot in the summer. Of the two-mile hike to his one-room country school. "In the winter," he related to me, "our teacher always had a wash basin of snow ready to treat our faces for frostbite!"

And he speaks of horse-and-wagon trips to Kerns Lake to fish; catching bass and bluegills which were preserved in salt for winter food.

At sixteen, after finishing the eighth grade, Nels struck out on his own, travelling to Odanah where he hoped to find a job in the Stearns Lumber Company's sawmill, cutting timber from the Bad River Indian Reservation. The mill was closed, and he went to work instead in a logging camp; his first job, but only one of many he was to have in the woods.

Having lived the life of a lumberjack, his tales are authentic; of life in the camps, the timber of the times, and the old-time equipment and tools used to harvest it. Yet, he is critical of the shortsightedness that turned the forest into quick cash, believing that, had better conservation been practiced, both the land and the people since would have gained.

Throughout his early years, Olson struggled to make a living; moving from place to place, seeking work wherever it could be found, at jobs that paid in most cases only a few cents an hour. And finally success in the Detroit, Michigan area where he and his two brothers, all skilled tradesmen, formed a company to build homes.

There, he met and married Frances, and in time, tired of big city life and yearning to return to his roots, they and their daughter, Karen, moved back to Mason.

In the years since, he and Frances have enjoyed life in their peaceful, beautiful surroundings. One of his hobbies has been collecting old tools, particularly old hammers. And he's done some wood carving.

But his greatest achievement, in my mind, has been his writing.

Two more books are in the making, he said. "I sit in the kitchen at night, and I write. Frances does all my typing. There are so many changes, we're thinking about a computer."

And to that I can only say — go for it, Nels! Like the rest of the things in your life!

Boots and Socks

I have this "thing" about boots and socks, and I know where it comes from. It goes back a long time, back to the 30s when I was a skinny, half-wild kid growing up in the country. Back in those days, what outdoor clothing that you could afford wasn't worth very much. Today's lightweight, insulated synthetics are much better.

So, as I remember, I went around most of the winter with cold feet.

But, then, it was at least partly my own fault. I remember clearly a trip to the shoestore for my winter footwear. The rage with all of us boys a that time was High-Cuts. High-Cuts were unlined leather knee-length boots, and they were next to worthless. But my buddies and I all had to have a pair.

Those were depression-era days and the shoe people weren't dummies. They built some smart sales appeal into their boots.

On the side of the right boot of each pair, there was a neat little leather sheath which contained a cheap jack-knife. Everyone knows that every country boy has to have a jack knife. I was no different. I just had to have that jack knife, and I wasn't about to settle for anything else.

With a forelorn look on their faces, my parents gave in. And I suffered with cold feet all winter.

Socks weren't much better. The cheap cotton variety

was common. If you were lucky, an aunt or grandmother would knit you a pair of genuine wool ones as a Christmas present.

And so it was in later years, that I grew to appreciate good boots and socks, especially socks. I have two dresser drawers crammed full of good-grade wool winter socks.

There's only one problem. One drawer is filled with neatly-folded, perfectly matched beauties. There are grey ones with red tops, white ones with green tops, and solid red and green ones.

The other drawer is a different story. No two match. And this is where the mystery comes in.

In between the clothes chute and my dresser drawers are the washer and dryer. Dirty socks go down the clothes chute, and Momma deposits them in the washer. Two socks go in; but two socks don't always come out. And I end up with a hodge-podge of orphan socks.

I've pondered this mysterious situation for a long time now, and I'd like to have someone explain to me how a wool sock eighteen inches long and weighing a pound can disappear into thin air — or thin water for that matter. But they do.

I've asked Momma, but she can't explain it to me either.

One of these days, that washer-dryer combo is going to give out. And when they do, I'm going to take them apart. I'm expecting to find a regular mother lode of my long-missing wool socks.

The situation used to frustrate me, but the problem doesn't bother me all that much anymore. I've resolved it you see. I've taken to wearing a gray one with a red top on one foot and a white one with a green top on the other foot.

So far, no one has questioned me about this bizarre behavior. But if anyone does, I'll just say I'm color-blind.

After all, there's really only one person that you have to please in this world, and that's yourself. And besides, they're just as warm that way.

A Tough and Hardy Breed

Late July, early August. . .this time of the year seems to always bring back a few memories of farm women in my life, back when I was a youngster. Right about now, as the crops ripen on our farms, recollections of the parts my mother, grandmothers, and aunts played each summer in the harvesting activities come sifting back.

Long hours and a mountain of hard work, that's what the women knew.

Take gardening, for instance. The farms, I recall back then, were almost totally self-sufficient. Not much food was bought at "the store." Thus, big gardens were the rule; lots of peas and beans, carrots, beets, plenty of tomatoes, and usually a strawberry and raspberry patch too.

And by August, the bounty from the earth would be building! Yet in those 1930 times, the home freezer, upon which most of us depend so heavily today, didn't exist. In fact, in my home country back then, the electricity that runs the things didn't even exist.

So, the ladies would start to talk about "canning time." And an annual frenzy of preserving fruits and vegetables for the winter ahead would begin. Down from the attic would come the pressure cooker, a machine that had an aura of danger attached to it, warnings of how they could explode as they huffed and puffed on wood-burning kit-

chen ranges.

Up from the basement would come boxes of blue Mason jars, the kind with a name embossed on their sides. Today they've become collector items at flea markets. The jars and their grey metal lids would be boiled, to sterilize, and a fresh supply of sealing rings, made of red rubber laid out.

From the garden would come the bushel baskets of tomatoes and the milkpails of peas. And for days on end, it seemed, the ladies would toil in their kitchens, steaming and hot in ninety-degree summer temperatures.

At the end of the day, long rows of shiny and glistening jars of freshly canned vegetables, would rest on clean dish towels on the kitchen table; waiting for their lids to pop, the signal that they'd cooled sufficiently and could be taken to the wooden shelves in the basement for storage.

Mixed in with it all, would be the normal, daily duties of cooking and serving three meals for the menfolks, who were busy putting up a second crop of alfalfa, and keeping an eye on the young kids.

Poultry raising was often another of the ladies' jobs. Each summer, my grandmother grew a sizeable number of chickens, ducks, geese, and occasionally, a turkey or two. The job started in the spring with her setting hens; went from clutches of fluffy chicks and ducklings trailing behind the old clucking hens, to plump full-feathered birds as the summer wore on.

Each evening before dark, she'd make her rounds to inspect her flock. First to the henhouse to gather the eggs from her leghorns in a peach basket she carried on her arm; eggs she sold for a little private income of her own. Then on to the fenced pens to assure that her other young charges had been properly fed and watered by my uncles.

And Grandma's weekends? Well, Saturdays, they didn't count. . .they were just another workday. Sundays? Well,

Sunday afternoons were the times when a passel of big city relatives always dropped in for a visit. . .and to stay for supper, of course.

And if it wasn't relatives stopping by, it would be a church picnic, an event where every lady in the parish was expected to pitch in. There'd be cakes and pies to be baked in advance. And on the big day, long hours spent peeling, boiling and mashing potatoes, frying a seemingly endless supply of chicken, and serving the hundreds that came to eat. And all in stifling hot kitchens, on hot summer days.

I think back today with great admiration to those long-ago farm women.

They were a tough and hardy breed.

Mary Kemen, the author's Grandmother, tends her flock in the early 1900's.

Marian Becker fishes in Beaver Dam Lake near Cumberland in the 1930's.

Vacations with Uncle Aneus and Aunt Mary

"We thought about it and planned for it all year," my wife said to me recently. July had brought back memories of camping trips she'd taken with her folks and brothers back in the 1930's.

"Write a column for me!" I told her. A story is always best when it comes directly from the teller's mouth. But I couldn't talk her into it. Momma, you see, is a smidgeon on the shy side.

"The car would be packed the night before," she told. "It was full of stuff — bedding, tent, groceries, clothing. Bamboo canepoles were tied on the side. Every spare spot was filled with something. Once, I remember, we stopped for a rest. And when the car door was opened, the coffee pot rolled down the road."

Each July, her dad received his one-week vacation from his job. And he sacrificed that week to take his family up north, to camp and fish, to visit their Uncle Aneus and Aunt Mary Peterson at their farm near Cumberland.

"I was just a little girl, maybe six or seven years old," Momma continued. "My brothers, Doug and Wes, were like fourteen and ten."

The trip from Kenosha would take all day. "The roads were narrow and bumpy. And it seemed like the weather was always hot. I remember the butter melting in the car," she noted.

"I rode in the bumpy backseat, and I dreaded the trip, because I always got carsick. When I started to turn green, they knew it was time to stop — what I wouldn't have given for Dramamine back then!"

The old-time Burma-Shave signs along the highways made the trip interesting. "They were fun, something to do. Read one and look forward to the next," she said. "When I began to see the orange Indian paintbrush flowers along the road, I knew we were getting close."

"We'd arrive at my uncle's farm in late afternoon. There was always a big welcome, because we were from the big city, and they didn't get many out-of-town visitors. My Uncle Aneus was a colorful character with a great sense of humor. I always looked forward to being around him, to hear his stories about living in the north."

The family camped in her uncle's yard. "We would hurry to get the tent put up and everything unpacked. Dad hated 'grit' on the floor of the tent, and he was forever sweeping it out. We slept on cots, and I remember one night being scared when a bear came around."

"The bugs, mosquitoes and deerflies, were bad. Back then, our only defense was a flyswatter, and that didn't help much," she added.

And, at last, the fishing. . . . .

"My uncle had a small lake on his property," she said. "What fun it was to go out on it and catch bluegills. And we'd have fresh fish for supper outside our tent."

But most of all, she recalls fishing trips to Beaver Dam Lake. "We rented a boat," she told. "Nobody owned boats back then. They were wooden, painted green, and seemed to always leak. You had to have a can along to bail with."

"We did a lot of canepole fishing, catching bluegills and small northerns. I used to say if a dragonfly sat on my bobber, it would bring me good luck."

"I was always afraid to put a worm on my hook. But one day, my brother Doug told me to either put on my own worms or I was done fishing. It took some time of terror, but I finally did it."

And catching bass. . .

"My brothers had a rod and reel and were catching bass on a Jitterbug. I was anxious to try, so they finally let me. My first few casts hit the weeds along shore, but then I got the knack. And that's when I remember the Jitterbug bobbing along, and the bass coming up to nab it. They were medium-sized, but they seemed like whales to me. They were my first big fish, and I was proud of them."

Evenings were spent visiting with Uncle Aneus and Aunt Mary. "They had a small, comfortable house with big trees in their yard. I remember the old-fashioned kitchen and a big old rocking chair. What a treat it was to sit in it after the tent. The grownups talked, comparing life styles. It seemed like a world apart!"

The week passed too quickly, and soon it was time to pack for the long trip home.

"We'd get home, tired and sunburned," Momma noted. "My mother loved flowers, and she'd go around checking her flowerbeds. The lawn would need cutting, and after unpacking, my dad would get out his old-fashioned push lawnmower."

A family vacation was over for another year.

"Looking back now," Momma concluded, "it was a lot of work and sacrifice for my parents.

"And little did I realize back then, that I'd be spending all of my adult life 'up north'."

. . . where the Indian paintbrushes still bloom in July.

The Funnies

I know now that I'm getting old. I don't understand the funnies anymore.

Recently, my bigtown Sunday paper dropped one of my very favorite comic strips. *"Snuffy Smith"* was its title. And in its place, came another of those super-sophisticated jobs, so high falooten' that it goes right over my head.

I've been watching the Letters to the Editor, to see if anyone else misses ole Snuf. But, so far, it looks like I'm a minority of one, mourning the passing of the old moonshine-making, card-cheating, chicken-thievin' cuss.

I've meditated a few times about why we have funny pages in our newspapers. Space costs money. And really, what do comic strips contribute? Yet, I've never seen a daily or a Sunday paper that didn't carry them.

I have to assume that the media people know well what they're doing. Apparently the public reads newspapers for more than the news. I'm no expert, but comics are part of what I call "balance", some soft reading to offset the hard stuff.

Snuffy Smith and I go back together about fifty years. Around the time I started to read pretty good, say third or fourth grade, I'd roll out of the sack in the dawn's early light and pad my way, barefoot, down our farm driveway to the mailbox. There I'd find, half-rolled-up, our big city Sunday paper.

Back in the house I'd go and sort through the thick stack until I found the funnies, the only section printed in color. Over each strip I'd pore, enjoying them as only a plain and simple country kid locked in a small world, could.

We had some good funnies in those days. I could understand all of them.

Take the Katzenjammer Kids, for instance. Two brothers of German extraction, and always in trouble. I could easily relate to them as they played their mischief and paid their price.

Then there were Maggie and Jiggs. Talk about battered wives! Old Jiggs was the original battered husband. Come home late from a night down at the club, and Maggie would greet him at the door with a barrage of cups and saucers. And if that wasn't enough, she'd bounce her rolling pin off his noggin. Outrageous, yet hilarious!

And Popeye, the Sailor, with his slow-moving sidekick, Wimpy. Wimpy had an addiction for hamburgers. Every once in a while, he'd have to have a fix of steaming, juicy burgers.

Popeye had a habit, too; spinach. Let his sweetheart, Olive Oyle, get kidnapped by the ruthless villian, Fagan! Old Popeye would pop the top of a can of spinach; gulp it down, and when his bicep muscles had swelled to their proper proportions, he'd beat the tar out of the culprit, to the hugs and kisses of his sweetie.

Flash Gordon! Here was pure fantasy. Imagine anyone dumb enough to think of men flying around in space in rocketships, with streams of fire jetting from their tails. Pure poppycock!

But old Snuffy Smith was my favorite. How I loved the old reprobate; his loyal, hard-working wife, Loweesy, and their kids, Judhead and Tater. I wish I could count the chuckles and laughs they gave me.

For fifty years, poor Loweesy suffered in their hillbilly mountain cabin, with a roof that poured water every time it rained. There she'd be, changing Tater's diaper as the rain dripped down into her pots and pans.

For fifty years, that "shifless skonk," Snuffy, never raised a finger to fix that roof. There he'd lay, on the bed, resting after an all night cardgame over at Lukey's place; his jug of corn squeezins brewed in his still back in the woods, where the "revenooers" couldn't find it, beside him.

Many's the time I clipped a strip and magnetted it to the frig door for Momma to read. Strips, showing Loweesy and her neighbor chum, Elviney, jawing over the gossip fence. "Tongue waggin," Snuf called it, over new hats or how the Widder Jones had run off with the new preacher. Outrageous, but hilarious!

So, I'm grieving the passing of my lifelong Sunday morning friends. It hurts to be a minority of one.

But I'll heal. There's another unscrupulous cad, you see. Hagar, The Horrible. He's a fearless Viking that periodically sacks England, yet has to have his "blankie" when he goes to bed at night. Poor Helga, his wife, has to scrub his ears when he's finally forced to take a bath.

Good old Hagar will help ease my pain. As Snuffy would say, he's a "bodacious" kind of a guy.

Deak's Hill

Deak's Hill laid a scant half-mile crosslots from my country farm home. Deak's Hill was my sledding hill. Come the first snows of November, Saturdays found me and the other neighborhood kids gathered there.

Created by the glaciers that carved southern Wisconsin 10,000 years ago, the hill couldn't have been constructed better for sledding, or "sleigh riding" as we called our winter play.

A natural opening in the woods, the hill stood barren of trees, stumps and boulders. Its farmer owner pastured his Holsteins on it. And by late autumn, when the cows were moved to his barn, the slope was left neatly clipped, ideal for sledding.

The hill's top had a gentle downhill taper, perfect for strong-legged farm kids to get a good running start for belly-flopping. Then, at its brow, it pitched sharply downward, to add acceleration to our slide.

And down at its base, the terrain flattened onto a smooth meadow, ideal for our final coasting to a stop. And for measurements of the "record" run for the day.

The times were the 1930's, a period when country kids lived simply, content to create their own fun. Today, I shake my head as I witness the highly-organized, regimented recreation of youngsters, void of creativity and spontaneity.

Let the first snowflakes swirl from a sodden sky, and my buddies and I would dig our sleds out of machine sheds and haymows. Inside ourselves, excitement burned at the prospect of exhilarating rides awaiting us on Deak's Hill.

Our old sleds weren't fancy, mostly paintless hand-me-downs from uncles who'd outgrown them. An inspection would be given each, maybe a new piece of clothesline tied to the front to replace one chewed by mice.

Next came the runner sharpening. Rusted from months of idleness, the steel had to be polished to bare metal brightness. Rusty runners cut speed and distance. And for hours, we'd pass the sled back and forth through a tub of furnace ashes until the runners glistened.

To be sure, somewhere in the neighborhood was always a youngster fortunate to have received a new "Flexible Flyer" for Christmas the year before. How we envied the lucky one, as we eyed the bright red paint, the shiny varnished maple. And above all, the flex of the wooden steering crosspiece. Such a sled would certainly do wonders on Deak's Hill.

Saturday afternoons found a veritable parade of youngsters moving along the town roads, coming from all directions, towing their sleds behind them. Mainly boys, but a lot of girls, too. Kids of all ages and sizes; dressed in sheepskin coats, Mackinaws, high-cut boots, and four-buckle overshoes. All headed for Deak's Hill.

Faced to the north, our hill's precious snow was shielded from the winter sun. And as one after another, we flew down its bank, the snow compacted into an ice-like raceway. Add a couple of inches of fresh white stuff to its surface, and the frozen track took on the speed of greased lightning.

The challenge, of course, was to see who could fly the fastest and finish the farthest. Run as fast as you can, leap airborne, and land atop your sled. Gather speed as you approach the brink, hang on tight, and listen to the cold air whistle past your ears; feel the sting of slivers of snow streaming from the runners against your face; plummet downward at what seemed, to a ten-year-old, to be breakneck speed.

At the toe of the slope, there'd be an abrupt breathtaking change of pace as the forces of gravity were overcome. Onto the level meadow we sped, and finally, the slow deceleration as we glided to a halt.

Laughter and shouts of glee would ring in the air, triumphant testimony to a thrilling ride. And a slow climb back up to do it all over again.

I drove by Deak's Hill awhile ago. It's still there. But the new houses and the modernistic church now nearby, tell me that it's doubtful that kids slide there anymore.

Wistfully, I gazed at the slope, the echoes and visions of winter days long past flowing back in my mind.

Somehow the old hill seemed smaller, not as steep, not as fearsome. And I wondered why.

The hill certainly hadn't changed. And then I knew. It is I that has.

It is I that has climbed too many bigger hills since.

Koichi Okubo

December 7, 1941! I'd been to a movie that Sunday afternoon. Returning, I walked through the front door of our house. In the living room, my father sat, his head glued to the old-fashioned Philco console radio of the day.

"The Japanese have attacked Pearl Harbor," he said, the shock lining his face. I was the oldest of his five sons, going on 15.

The day marked the beginning of a deep impact on my life. One by one, I watched older baseball and fishing buddies leave for military duty. And too often I watched as little flags with gold stars appeared in front-room windows. Stars for friends I'd never see again.

And, inside me, a deep hatred for Japan began to grow.

Then finally, my turn. At 17, I'd enlisted in what was called the Air Force Reserve. A year later, a young kid barely 18, I was called to active duty.

The war in Europe was freshly over. Germany had surrendered. But in the Pacific, the carnage raged on. Then, on a hot day in August of 1945, the word reached us at Keesler Field, Mississippi, that the Japanese, too, had quit.

The end of the shooting generated confusion. No longer would we be trained to be pilots, navigators and bombardiers. My destiny would change. I'd be a weatherman. And, off to meterology school at Chanute Field, Illinois I was shipped.

Three months later, I found myself aboard a troop ship looking up at the Golden Gate bridge. Ten more days found me carrying my barracks bag down the gang plank in the harbor at Manila.

It wasn't hard to see there'd been a war on. The harbor was dotted with broken hulks of half-sunken ships beginning to rust in the salty air.

What would be my fate, my job? Battle-weary GIs were heading home. More like us were coming in to replace them, to take over "occupation" duties.

There were six of us weather observers. Rumors flew. Some said we were headed for the South Pacific where atomic bomb tests were planned. And for a couple weeks we sat around at Nichol's Field waiting for orders.

Then a decision. One dark night we were loaded aboard a C-54 transport plane, headed for Japan. We'd been assigned to the Air Force weather station at Atsugi Air Base outside Tokyo, General MacArthur's home base.

And there at Atsugi, I met Koichi Okubo.

The Atsugi weather station was manned by Japanese meteorologists conscripted by the American forces. Some twenty in number, my job would be to supervise these Japanese nationals, to assure that weather data would be gathered 24-hours-a-day all the way from Australia to Alaska.

How would I relate to these people; men that represented the enemy, humans I'd learned to hate?

Once more, my life began to change. Okubo changed it.

A roly-poly congenial man with a constant cherubic smile on his face; slowly but surely we became close friends. And the hard emotions inside me toward the Japanese people began to soften.

The months passed. Our work went well. More Americans came to replace the Japanese meteorologists.

One by one they left to return to the Central Meteorological Observatory, Japan's weather service.

And finally Okubo's turn. As he said his goodbye, he handed me a letter. I read it and tucked it into my shirt pocket. Our friendship was ending.

Then a day in November of 1946, my duty too was finished. Once more, I found myself carrying my barracks bag, this time to board a train that would take me to a ship. And home.

As the train began to move slowly out of the station, I took my last look at Japan. The strains of Les Brown's *"Sentimental Journey"* flowed from the loudspeakers. Little Japanese boys and girls lined the tracks, waving tiny paper American flags.

I was leaving; going home, a different person.

In the breast pocket of my Ike jacket, rested Okubo's letter. I took it out and read it one more time. I've saved that letter these past 43 years. This is what my Japanese friend, in his pidgin-English, wrote:

"To Dear American Observers:

I shall come back to C.M.O. at first of next month. I could work pleasantly with you at Atsugi after I shall come back to C.M.O.

Every time I meet U.S. Army, you will come to my mind. I mean to work in C.M.O., and I expect the new Japan. I thank you for your kindness for long time.

Now it is winter. As it become cold gradually, please hold good health. Good-bye—

Koichi Okubo"

Okubo, I trust you found the "new Japan." You helped me find a new self.

Long Lake Full of Logs

Doug Todd and I met one afternoon last summer at a neighborhood gathering. "Come out and see me sometime," he'd said, "I'll tell you about the old logging days around Long Lake."

I drove into his yard the other day, parked the truck, and knocked on his door. Surrounding his home was a grove of tall white pine trees, trees like those that shaped his past. I waited a minute or two, and he opened the door.

"Come on in," he said. "You've got to excuse me for being so slow at answering the door. I'm slow at getting around." Todd, you see, is 77, and he's had surgery on both of his knees. He walks with a cane.

"How about a cup of coffee?" he asked. And we sat down for a good visit. "This house was built in 1916," he continued. "My dad sawed the lumber for it from pine logs he fished from the bottom of Muskrat Bay on Long Lake. I've lived here since I was four years old. The floor used to have so many knot holes in it that once a bird flew in here."

Todd's father was a logger back in the virgin timber days of the early 1900's, times when vast stands of white pine covered eastern Washburn County.

"Dad went to work in the woods when he was fourteen. He was called a 'swamper'. He chopped limbs from the big pines with an axe after they were cut. My grandfather was a teamster, driving six-horse teams. And my grandmother cooked in logging camps, camps that had as many as 160 men."

Three lumber companies were cutting the pines in those early days, Todd said; the Rice Lake Lumber Company, the Knapp Stout Lumber Company, and the St. Croix Lumber Company.

"The logs were moved on the water. The lakes and rivers were our roads back then," he noted. The logs were hauled on sleighs in the winter and unloaded onto the ice.

"The St. Croix Company put its logs into Crystal Brook. Then they went through Spooner Lake into the Yellow River to the Namekagon and the St. Croix, to their sawmill at St. Croix Falls."

"The Rice Lake and Knapp Stout companies drove their logs down Slim Creek. It had three dams on it. The dam that now holds the Slim Creek Flowage was built on an old logging dam site."

"Then the logs were floated into the upper end of Long Lake. Some logs were sleighed directly to the lake at what's called Klondike Landing. My dad saw Long Lake so full of pine logs that you could walk across it in the spring."

The floating logs were moved down the lake in large booms to the Brill River, eighteen miles south, at the lake's outlet.

"Knapp Stout had a steam tug to pull its booms. But the Rice Lake Lumber Company used manpower. They had an eight-man bateau and a two-man bateau. The two-man boat would move ahead and drop a large anchor. The eight-man boat had two 'jennies' mounted on it, one on each end. The crew would then hand winch the bateau and logs forward by winding in the cable attached to the anchor."

The logs went down the Brill River to the Red Cedar,

and into Rice Lake. "There they were separated. All the logs were stamped to show who owned them. The Knapp Stout logs continued down the Red Cedar to their mill at Menominee."

Todd tells other tales of those early pioneer days.

"My Uncle Monroe was a fiddle player, and my Uncle George was a 'caller'. Uncle Charlie played the organ. The three played at wakes in the Irish settlement between here and Rice Lake. What parties they used to have!"

"But Uncle Monroe broke his arm cranking a Model T Ford. And after that, he couldn't get the tunes out of his violin any more."

Todd remembers when the main street of Rice Lake was paved with blocks of wood standing on end. "I saw it when I was twelve years old. They were rough to ride over."

And he recalls the bad forest fires that burned through the area, fires that burned deep into the ground, smoldering in the roots of the pine stumps.

Following the pine logging, Todd's father became a caretaker for the summer cottages that were springing up on Long Lake. "Dad quit caretaking in 1958, and I took over. I started with ten places; and when I quit in 1979, I had 55," he said. "I still keep a watch on some of them." Some of the early summer homes, built with pine logs hand-hewn with broad axes, still stand today.

Doug Todd told me a lot more — things about the early farming days; of the one-room school he went to; how he rescued the young lady teacher who had sunk to her neck in a snow drift while walking to their schoolhouse one morning after a blizzard. Stories I'll long remember.

Doug Todd, you see, is a genuine pioneer; a walking history book. One that still gets around — with the help of a cane.

Winter Mornings

I stand before my dining room window these January mornings and gaze into the darkness of the backyard. Daylight doesn't come until almost eight o'clock these days. And I watch the world slowly, gradually, turn from black to white.

I'm sure there are many who hate these late winter mornings. Momma's one. She's a brightness-oriented person. Give her a dark day, and she reacts. "This weather's the pits," she'll announce and flip on all the lights in the house.

Not I. I find the gentle softness of semi-darkness a soothing respite from the nerve-jangling stimulation of brightness. And I tell her so. "Opposites attract!" she'll come back, shaking her head in dismay.

The backyard is a thing of beauty on these dark early mornings, especially if the wind isn't blowing. The scene is still and peaceful, serene, as a new page in the book of life awaits to be written.

Against a western sky, almost imperceptibly changing to silver, the windbreak of pines and spruces stands black, silhouetted. The wood pile looks husky and solid against the snow, beginning to gray in the gathering light. Like an artist's work done in charcoal, the portrait is slowly painted by Mother Nature's hand; subtle, soft strokes gently caressing the outdoor canvas.

And I find my thoughts drifting back to mornings on country farms long ago; times when I peeked through cracks in barn doors and watched cold dawns break on horizons to the east.

I suppose I was six, maybe seven; in first grade, maybe second; just beginning to become aware of the workings of the world around me.

My grandfather would begin the day by banging an old wrench on the old-fashioned cast iron steam radiator in his bedroom. "The Boss" his six sons and three daughters called him. The clang of his pounding travelled throughout the house, from bedroom to bedroom, a signal that the time had come to roll out of bed and begin the day's tasks.

Dressing, I'd follow my uncles downstairs to the huge kitchen, the center of all family activity. There, my grandmother would already have the methane-fueled gas lights glowing and a fire crackling in her wood-burning cooking range.

In a huddle in a corner, my uncles slipped into their blue-denim barn jackets, pulling four-buckle rubber boots over their work shoes, and as each stepped out the back door, he picked up a shiny stainless steel milk pail. A couple of kerosene lanterns would be lit, and into the cold darkness we marched; the snow crunching and squeaking underfoot, the swinging lanterns casting a moving panorama of pale yellow light and black shadows against the woodpile and trees.

The first stop was the windmill to test the long-handled pump. Was it frozen? Maybe a teakettle of hot water would be retrieved from the kitchen to free its innards.

Then through a wooden barn door, creaking in complaint to the cold, past the pens of young stock and the bull, looking menacing with a big copper ring in his nose. And into the cow barn.

The animals expected us, almost glad to see us. Those lying resting in their straw bedding would rise to their feet, others bellowing their good-mornings.

The lanterns were hung from spikes driven into the wooden-beamed rafters, their glow reflecting from the whitewashed ceiling. Taking their three-legged milking stools from wooden pegs on the wall, my uncles would settle beside contented Holsteins, and begin their morning milking.

Ping-ping-ping, the streams of milk would echo from the sides of the steel pails held between their knees, gradually changing to a soft squish-squish as the pail began to fill.

Silently, mysteriously, a motley bevy of cats, big and small, would sift in from their nests in the hay mow, the first rewarded with a well-aimed stream of milk direct from the cow into its opened mouth. The rest fed at a small wooden trough from the first pail of milk.

From cow to cow, my uncles moved; their milk poured into tall milk cans through a large-mouthed strainer with a fresh clean cotton filter in its bottom. And when the job was done; outside the half-light of the new day would have arrived.

Today, I ponder those old times as I stand before my window in the morning darkness. People knew hard work. People knew not modern conveniences.

My hand reaches for the light switch; and in an instant, those memories are dimmed, darkened by the brightness that suddenly floods the room.

Christmas Vacations

"Christmas vacation," we always called this time of year as kids, back in my school days, when we'd get a week or so off from our studies about now. And Christmas vacation, it's still called today.

For some reason this year, I find myself looking back to those old days. I really can't say why. Maybe it's the easy winter we've experienced so far, the mild days and the light snow on the ground. Somehow, I'm reminded of similar times when Christmas vacations meant a brief freedom from books and desks, a chance to have some fun in the outdoors, to do boy stuff.

A lot of good memories come back.

Like the very first I recall, Christmas breaks as a youngster in my early grades, when I was six , seven , eight years old. Out to my grandfolks' farm I'd be sent, to spend some time, to get better acquainted with granddad, grandmother and a bevy of aunts and uncles.

Late December was wood-making time for grandpa. And there, in his woodlot, I got my first taste of timber and logging. There, in the company of my uncles, I learned to swing an axe, to pull a cross-cut saw, and to drive a wedge; skills and feelings for trees that stayed with me all of my life.

There'd be some hunting. What a thrill I'd know as I trailed along behind my Uncle Amy, the best outdoorsman in the family and a very good man with a shotgun and rifle, as he poked along brushy fence rows, to kick out a cotton-tail rabbit or two. Dressed out, the critters would be hung to freeze on the back porch. And when my vacation was over, and I left for home, proudly I carried them along.

As the years passed, and I grew older and more independent, Christmas vacations began to take on a different meaning. A cluster of friends gradually formed, neighborhood buddies, youngsters of ten, twelve years of age.

Christmas vacation usually meant snow on the ground. And over at Deak's Hill, the gang of us would gather, to belly-flop our sleds down its steep slope, the runners of our American Flyers hissing and the wind created by our break-neck speed whistling in our ears.

Or to the little pond in Newman's woods, where with scoop shovels borrowed from our fathers' graneries, we'd clear the ice's surface. Then we'd sit on stumps or fallen trees to fasten our old-fashioned "clamp" skates to the soles of our shoes. Or, if you were one of the more fortunates, lace on a pair of brand-new "shoe" skates, a recent Christmas gift perhaps.

Hockey sticks would be contrived from crooked saplings, pucks of knotty chunks of wood. And for hours, we'd skate; slipping, sliding, tripping, falling, amid shouts of laughter and boisterous bravado.

Boyhood years passed into teenage years, however. And the play went out of Christmas vacation. On two sides of the world, a war raged. Life took on a deadly serious side, as one by one, I watched friends leave, several of whom I never saw again.

And ultimately a call of my own. I've never forgotten, as an eighteen-year-old, that furlough in 1945. Ahead an overseas assignment awaited. . .and that Christmas vacation became one of goodbyes.

Christmas vacations were never the same after that. Gone were boyhood interests, replaced with adult pursuits. Like the hitchhiking home from college in 1949 to slip a ring on the finger of a demure young lady with auburn bangs hanging down over her forehead; a ring she's worn ever since, for the more than forty-two years she's been at my side.

Christmas vacations have since been times of kids of our own; of them excitedly opening presents from under brightly-lighted trees, of winter travels together to visit and bond with their grandparents over checkerboards and jigsaw puzzles.

And in time, to watch as they too have moved out into the world, creating families of their own, and grandkids that bring joy to these Christmas vacations today.

Life, as Christmas vacations, goes on. And we're grateful.

A Happy New Year to all!

Some Hair-Raising Tales

George Young has seen his share of bear and moose.

George is a neighbor of mine, of sorts. He and his wife, Dorthea, live down the road a couple mail boxes from my tree farm over in the Stone Lake country.

Last summer, George had called me. "Stop in some time," he'd said. "I'll tell you some hair-raising tales." Now, when it comes to hair-raising tales, I'm always a ready listener. Yet, not being too swift in many ways, it took me until the other day, to take him up on his invitation.

George had just returned from delivering a load of firewood. I call him "The Firewood King." In his yard, neatly stacked, are always long piles of the stuff. And I asked him about the business. "Oh, last year we cut a little over 500 cords," he told me. Not bad for a man that's 75 and has had heart bypass surgery.

And with that casual dismissal of his accomplishment, he opened an old photo album. "These are pictures of the days back in the early fifties when I ran logging camps in the wilds of northern Minnesota. And it was wild!" he said.

"In all, I ran eight different camps for the J.C. Campbell and Kimberly Clark companies," he added. "I cut mostly spruce pulpwood."

His first camp had six men besides himself. "We were

batching it," he said. "I did the cooking. I didn't know much about it, but I took my wife's cookbook along, and I learned!" Later, Dorthea and his youngsters joined him.

The country abounded with game; deer, moose, bear, snowshoe rabbits, beaver and timber wolves. "You couldn't find a wilder place anywhere for animals than northern Minnesota at that time," Young said. "And the fishing was the same, big brook trout and northern pike."

At one of his camps, George had dug a large hole with his small bulldozer, a tractor for skidding logs. The hole was used as a dump for garbage and later covered. "There were always ten to fifteen bears there every night, both black and brown. We'd go over and watch them. They never bothered us, but we kept the kids away," he said.

The bears weren't to be overly-trusted, however. "One day, one of my cutters met a big one coming down a trail," Young recalls. "That bear wasn't backing up for anyone. If we weren't coming along behind, the man might have been killed."

Another time, George had gone to bed, leaving some groceries on the table of his small cabin. "I heard a noise on the porch," he explained. "I had a little two-cell flashlight, and I got up and shined it through the screen of a window. Woof! Right in my face! If you've ever seen a mother bear mad, she was. Her two cubs went up a tree, and she didn't want to leave. Finally, the cubs came down and she left."

Moose gave George and his crew some exciting moments too. "Across a swamp a half-mile, they had a rutting area. We'd hear the bulls fighting at night. They really tore up the earth. There'd be hair all over. You could go over there anytime and pick up moose horns."

"One day I heard the darndest hollering I've ever heard," he continued. "I went to check and found two of my cutters up a tree. A big bull moose was standing there, mad as heck.''

"Get him out of here!'' one of the cutters hollered.

"Well, you know, that son-of-a-gun treed me on top of my tractor,'' George said. "There I was, up on the end of the boom. It was Fall, rutting time, and he was ornery! Well, the cutters started their powersaws, and the moose finally left.''

Once, George tried to do a wounded moose a favor. The young bull had been attacked by a bear. "You could see what was wrong,'' George remembers. "It's back and hind quarters had been badly gouged.'' George and two of his men were considering roping the animal and cleansing its wounds.

"But he wasn't in that kind of a mood,'' George said. "Luckily there was a pulp pile between us and moose. I saw the hair come up on its back, and I hollered 'hit the pulp pile, Raymond.' The moose struck with its front feet and almost got him.''

Timber wolves were also seen. "We'd spot 'em. They never bothered us and we didn't them,'' George tells.

Young's adventures with wild animals did not lesson his love for them. If anything, that affection and respect are deeper today.

"I learned, when I met a bear or a moose, don't crowd 'em. It works. The more excited you get, the better chance they'll attack,'' he says.

Seems like bear and moose have a lot in common with some people.

Momma's Into Chickens

Chickens! They've come home to roost. No, there's no new henhouse out back with cackling hens and crowing roosters. They're in the kitchen.

Momma's into chickens. The whole thing started a couple months ago when she decided the kitchen needed a facelift. New wallpaper, she said the place needed. So after a couple weeks of agonizing over patterns, up went the wallpaper, chicken wallpaper.

Well, that wasn't enough. More chickens would be needed to match the motif. Next came new canisters for her sugar, flour, coffee and tea — cans with lazy-looking, contented chickens on the sides. Then new covers for her cake mixer and the toaster, quilted jobs with chicken faces on them.

On the wall, from a rummage sale, went a frumpy, full-size fowl with a little hangy-down sign that says "Welcome." And a ceramic hen sitting on a nest as a bookend to hold up her cookbooks. There's a brown burlap bird, complete with flowers embroidered on its sides and white lacy frills, reposing on top of the fridge.

In front of the radio sits an orange, knitted biddie with a fake egg inside of it. And in the drawers, are chicken potholders and chicken towels. There's even a happy hen, hatching on the cookie jar.

"What's with all the chickens?" I asked the other day.

"Chickens are in!" she said.

"In what?"

"They're country! Chickens are big. So are geese and pigs and black-and-white cows."

Now that's interesting, I thought. I figure I know a little bit about geese, pigs, cows and chickens. Especially chickens. I knew a Rhode Island Red when I saw one by the time I was in third grade. And leghorns, they were thick as flies.

There were always plenty of chickens around the farms I hung around as a youngster. My grandmother was very good at raising chickens. She always had a big flock around the place. And from her I got some first-hand lessons. All the way from watching the little downy darlings peck their way out of their shells to enter the world, to the crates of carefully cleaned eggs that stood in the cool of the back hall. Eggs that she hauled off to town to sell; "egg money" she called it, her private little kitty.

And on a Sunday afternoon, when more of the city relatives dropped by than were expected, one of my uncles and I would be dispatched to the chicken coop to snare a few fat fryers. A brief stop at the chopping block, some scalding water, feathers flying out by the woodpile, innards removed, and there were finger-lickin' drumsticks long before Colonel Sanders came along.

I even got into a fight with a chicken once. Just a tad, I couldn't have been more than seven or eight. My grandfather had a big rooster around the place, one of those orange Buff Orpingtons. The bird was a mean old buzzard, standing a good two feet tall. And it thought it owned the place.

Well, as I made my daily rounds around the farmyard checking on the calves and the bullheads in the stock tank, that miserable, ornery critter would put the run on me;

jumping at me, pecking my bare feet.

Finally I had enough, and I started carrying a broomstick. Sure enough, one day here comes that feisty, feathered fowl. Right up to me, wings outstretched, with blood in its eyes. Well, I planted both feet and when it got a broomstick length away, I wound up with a home run swing that would have made Babe Ruth proud. Whack! I caught that rotten rooster right alongside the head. Down it went, flopped a couple times, and it was all over.

Now, I thought, I'm in big trouble. Out of the corner of my eye I saw my grandfather's long legs striding across the barnyard. Yup, I'm sure gonna get it now. I've killed the rooster.

Well, as Gramp got closer I saw the big smile on his face. He'd seen the whole thing. And when I heard him laughing, the fear of punishment went out of me. Chuckling all the while, he picked up the tough old bird and went about the business of getting it ready for the roasting pan. As I recall, it was as tough in death as it was in life.

The other night I was lying in bed, half asleep. Momma had the bedroom TV on. All of a sudden I heard her exclaim, "Chickens!"

"Huh," I muttered.

"Chickens! Chicken cups! They're drinking from chicken cups!" she said.

"What's the big deal about chicken cups?" I asked.

"They're cute," she replied and snapped off the set.

Chickens! One more and I just might go "Brrawk!" One more and I just might never darken the door of Colonel Sanders again.

Aunt Kitty's Cuckoo Clock

Well, I've almost completed my annual springing ahead for daylight savings time. Around our place, that yearly ritual takes awhile. Sure, the first morning Momma sees to it that the kitchen clock gets kicked ahead an hour. But the rest take awhile, like maybe a couple weeks.

So I wander around the house, confused, asking "What's the right time?", as I ponder big hands and little hands, and red numbers staring at me from the digital next to the bed. And one of these days I'll get around to my wrist watches. Last will come the yellow-eyed creep on the dashboard of my truck, the one I always have to wade through the operator's manual in the glove compartment to set. Usually that's about August.

My recent clock caper reminded me of my Aunt Kitty, my godmother and a grand lady. She and my Uncle Jess had a big farm, maybe ten miles from our place. Good memories remain of summer sunday afternoons spent there.

Aunt Kitty always had a pony around for us kids to ride in her apple orchard, apples that fed a cider mill, near which the old folks gathered when the fruit was ripe. Aunt Kitty's place was always popular in cider season for some reason.

Her house was typical of the day. Two stories, two big porches, set in the middle of a big lawn where we played croquet, eight rooms as I remember; four on the first floor, a kitchen, dining room, living room, and parlor. High-ceilinged, with beautifully carved woodwork, the rooms were elegant.

And there, hanging prominently on the living room wall, was Aunt Kitty's cuckoo clock, tick-tocking as its pendulum swung methodically back and forth, marking the passage of time.

I loved that cuckoo clock. Not too sharp at telling time, not knowing exactly when that little yellow bird was about to pop out, I'd sit there on the floor, patiently waiting for that mystical, magical machine to perform its duties.

Aunt Kitty's cuckoo clock was the first timepiece in my life, as best I can recall. Many since have followed.

Like my grandfather's "alarm" clock. Gramp's home had steam heat. Each room had one of those old-fashioned cast-iron radiators. Come, say five o'clock in the morning, when it was time to milk the cows, he'd bang on his bedroom radiator with an old wrench. "Time to get moving," the metallic message said, as it travelled from room to room. Nobody needed a clock to tell what time it was.

My Uncle Allie taught me some time-telling, too.

Take a hot July morning, when I'd be helping hoe bull thistles out in one of Gramp's cornfields. My stomach (another timepiece of mine) would begin to ask if it wasn't time to eat.

"Uncle Allie, isn't it dinner time yet?" I'd ask. "Just a minute," he'd say and prop his hoe handle vertically in the air, solemnly studying its shadow on the bare soil. "Nope, only 11:30!" he'd answer, and back to chopping thistles we'd go.

Then, back in my basic training days with the Air Force, at the tail end of World War II, my barracks had a corporal who was a clock of sorts — the rat!

There my buddies and I would lie, snoring peacefully on two long rows of canvas cots. And from the pitch-black, pre-dawn darkness, in would waltz this power-mad two-striper, shouting obscenities at the top of his lungs, to roll us out of the sack.

Today, I wouldn't give that contemptuous corporal the time of day!

Through time, I've received a number of timepieces with more than a little sentimental value attached. Like the 1944 wristwatch my folks gave me upon my graduation from high school; a watch paid for with sacrifice, saving, and skimping.

And two birthday watches; watches I still wear, one from Momma, the other from daughter and her family.

There's the handsome, long-stemmed, gold pocketwatch with its long gold chain; a watch that you wind up and wear tucked into the vest of your Sunday suit like the old-timers did years ago. *"To Dad"* it says inside the back cover, a Christmas present from son.

All treasured, they stand for special times.

And yet, I find myself reminiscing back to that first; Aunt Kitty's cuckoo clock. How I wish it were hanging on my wall right now.

Maybe I'd set it for daylight savings time. And then maybe I wouldn't.

I really wouldn't care.

Collecting Cars

I was coming home the other night from the tree farm and there, neatly parked in a neighbor's yard, was a line-up of shiny old cars. Drive in, I thought, maybe there's a '51 Chev, my first new car, one I loved deeply.

And there I met Rick and Nancy Seckora. The Seckoras collect old cars. Right now they own twenty-five. But there'll probably be more.

"Some people go fishing, some go golfing," Rick said. "My enjoyment is collecting old cars. It's a hobby, not a business. I just think they should be saved. They're not for sale."

The Seckoras have some beauties; cars that represent an era when automobiles had individuality and distinctiveness, unlike the peas-in-a-pod lookalikes of today. A car must be at least twenty years old to qualify for collector status.

"Every one has a story behind it," Rick continued. "That 1946 Oldsmobile over there was the car my dad and mother had their first date in. My grandfather gave it to me when I was fourteen. I had to cut some trees to get it out of the woods."

"The wheel rims, tires, and hubcaps were gone, but I looked around and found everything. I used to drive it back and forth to high school."

"And that '54 Pontiac Star Chief convertible — it came

from within twenty miles of Nancy's home in North Dakota.''

Rick likes cars with high performance engines. "I'm into 'muscle' cars. I like them because they don't make cars like that any more. I like to open the hood and see nothing but motor and carburetors.''

A special example is his 1970 Plymouth Cuda. "It was called a 440 Six Pack when it came out of the factory,'' he said. "It's got three carburetors under a ram-air hood. It's rated at 390 horsepower. Only 868 were built.''

"We bought it from a family whose son had owned it. He was killed in Vietnam, and his folks hung on to it for quite awhile after that.''

A white Cadillac convertible had caught my eye, a sleek symbol of the elegance of its time. "It's a '64,'' Rick said. "Nancy and I were riding around Houston, Texas one day, and she spotted it. We drove in, and sure enough, it was for sale.''

"The lady cried when we drove it away,'' Nancy added.

Twenty of the cars were collected while the Seckoras lived in Houston. "Except for one or two we brought up by trailer, we drove all of them here on our vacations,'' she said.

Today, the cars are stored in a large metal garage which doubles as their workshop. Nancy enjoys working with Rick on the restoration and maintenance.

"She's helped pull motors,'' Rick said. "And, last spring, we changed the oil on 22 of them one day.''

"The first thing I do is clean the car inside and out. Then I pull the wheels, check the brakes, steering and transmission. I give it a good overhaul. You've got to have good tools,'' he said.

And which is Nancy's favorite? "That '72 Oldsmobile Cutlass convertible!'' she replied. "It's special because

Rick fixed it up for me. I call it my little white cream puff."

I asked where they locate missing parts. "We spend a lot of time in junk yards," they answered. "Those are fun days. Hayward's got a good junk yard. We spend whole days up there!"

The Seckoras display their cars. Each is driven at least five miles a year. "And we bring some to the Spooner Car Show," Rick said. "Last year we had ten there. This year I don't know. It'll be up to Nancy as to how many she wants to clean and wax."

The show is sponsored by the Badger Studebaker Club. This year it will be held June 10 at the Spooner Fairgrounds. Last year over one hundred cars were displayed.

Collector cars are identified by blue license plates. "The first license costs $60, any additional are $40. But the plates are good as long as we own the cars," Rick said.

The Seckoras have met many "super nice" people in their car dealings, they say. "Then people drive in the yard to look at the cars. We feel it's just good country hospitality," Rick commented.

"The opening day of fishing season, three gentlemen from the Twin Cities were going fishing and saw the cars. They drove in and spent a half-hour looking at them," Nancy noted.

Even her black and white cat gets into their auto act. "His name in Bondo," Nancy explained, named after a product used to fill dents in car bodies.

Talk with the Seckoras and their deep affection for their car collection shows. "They all have significance behind them," Rick said. "You feel satisfaction in their restoration."

"We rattle off these cars like they're our children!"

Nancy added.

I know the feeling. If I ever see a '51 Chev parked in their yard, in I'll drive. And I'll give it a big hug.

Old Bottles

I was wading up one of my favorite trout streams the other day, the stream I call "the beautiful lady." The day was rotten for trout fishing, the sun beaming down from a cloudless sky through the still leafless trees on the banks. Fishing was poor.

But, what the heck, I was having fun visiting with the lady, checking on how she'd made it through the winter.

And there, at the tail of a deep pool, where I usually catch a trout, in the gin-clear water, I saw the outline of a bottle lying on her bottom. An old beer bottle, I figured.

Now it's unusual to find a beer bottle on the bottom of a trout stream. Beer cans, pop cans, yes. Bottles, no.

The old bottle looked interesting lying there in the thigh-deep water, covered with green-black scum. Obviously, it'd been there a long time. Perhaps, over winter, the lady's current had washed away the years of silt to expose it.

Check it out, I told myself. And with the toe of my boot, I carefully eased it toward the bank. With each nudge of my foot, a dark cloud of muddy water rose from the bottom. And I'd have to wait a few seconds for the water to clear, to locate the bottle again. Which probably spooked the trout in the hole. Which is probably why I didn't catch any.

But finally, I moved the bottle into the shallows where I

could reach it. And I picked it up, rubbed my hand over its surface to rinse off the crud that coated it, and shook out the black gunk from its innards. Yup! It was a good one.

I'm a bottle collector of sorts, you see. Empty ones, that is. And the older, the better. Not that I go searching for bottles. I'm not into collecting that far. But if, in my ramming around in the boondocks, I find one that looks like it's got some history, I'll drag it home. I suppose I've got close to a hundred I've found, or been given, over the years.

Nor am I an expert on bottles, like the people that are avid collectors. I know just enough to let me recognize things that tell that a bottle comes from an era long past.

For instance, the old bottle I held in my hand there in the trout stream had its identifying label embossed in the glass. Not like the smooth ones with glued paper labels that we see today.

"Ren" or "Resc Beer, Duluth," it read in fancy script. Does anybody know of an old-time brewery in Duluth that would fit that description? I'd sure like to hear.

The old bottle will join others on shelves in the basement cubbyhole where I retreat to do my pen-pushing.

There it'll stand beside others that read "Ashland Brewing Co."; "Schmidt St. Paul, Minn."; "Fitger Duluth"; "Christian Moerlein Brewing Co. Cincinnati, O."; and "Columbia Brewing Co. Logansport, Ind.".

It'll rest with ancient soda bottles. Like the one that says "Spooner Bottling Works" that has a spoon embossed on its glass side. And the truly beautiful pale blue bottle that reads "Phillips Bottling Works Phillips, Wis." Another with the words "T.F. Mackmiller Iron River, Wisc." And an oldie that says simply "Cloquet Club" with a crooked seam down its side, marketed undoubtedly out of Cloquet, Minnesota many years ago.

It'll join old booze bottles with "Old Quaker", "H and A Gilbey Gin", and "House of Lords Whiskey" stamped on them. There'll be a few with eagles, wings outstretched, and some with no names or emblems at all; relics probably from the Prohibition days of the 20's, when bootleggers didn't want to be identifiable.

There'll be a couple dozen old medicine bottles of all shapes and sizes. Like the beauty that reads "Syrup of Hypophosphites Fellows" which, in its day, was probably a cure-all for everything from in-grown toe nails to summer misery. And the green-tinted bottle that states "Pluto Water America's Physic", that I found on an island in Pipe Lake in Polk County.

I like old bottles. I pick one up, and I find myself wondering about the person who threw it away. What kind of a person was he or she? What was on his or her mind when the bottle was casually cast aside?

For someone, many years ago, an old bottle was only trash. But today, for me, it's a peek into the history of humanity.

For me, old bottles are time-worn treasures.

Tell Me About Oats!

Seems like I can't pick up a magazine or turn on the TV anymore without somebody telling me about whole grain health foods.

Oats is the latest miracle munch. Eat oats and you'll feel your oats, they say. Tell me about oats!

I'm an expert on oats. I grew up with oats. I've planted oats, weeded oats, cut oats, shocked oats, thrashed oats, bagged oats, shovelled oats, fed oats to horses. And above all, I've eaten plenty of oats.

That's why I hate oats. I don't care if oats is good for my pituitarity gland or anything else. You can have your oats.

Back when I was a kid, oats was big. My folks raised a lot of oats. Come May, my grandfather would say, "Well, it's time to sow the oats."

Come June, when the stuff was knee-high, he'd hand me a long-handled hoe and say, "Bob, go cut those bullthistles out there in the oats field." And there I'd stand all day, under my straw hat, in the hot sun, chopping those miserable thistles!

I got my first real job because of oats. I was twelve. Gramp hired me to be his blower man on the thrashing machine he took around the neighborhood every August. There I'd sit all day, on top of the machine, amidst whirling pullies and churning belts, blowing oats straw into neat strawstacks.

Fifty cents a day I got. That is, when I could collect. Those old German farmer neighbors were tighter than the bark on a scrub oak.

No wonder I hate oats.

And, when I wasn't making strawstacks, Gramp would stick me in the grain bin. "Bob, today you're going to shovel back the oats," he'd tell me.

So, up the ladder to the oats bin I'd crawl. There I'd sit with my shovel, as a steady stream of stupid oats flowed up to me from the thrashing machine. There I'd sit in the dark all day, my mouth covered with my red bandana handkerchief to keep the clouds of dust out of my lungs. There I'd sit, shoveling that no-good oats into the far corners of the bin.

Slowly the walls would close in on me. And steadily that rotten oats would begin to swallow me. First, up to my knees. Then my waist. And when it was about to my Adam's apple, Gramp would poke his head in to check on me.

If the bin wouldn't hold another single, solitary shovelful, he'd say, "Well, I guess you can come down now."

Thanks a bundle, Gramp! No wonder I've got claustrophobia.

Then there were my oatmeal breakfasts. Come cold winter mornings, and down the stairs from my bedroom I'd race, to slip into longjohns and highcuts by the pot-bellied stove. In the kitchen, my mother would be whipping up a big batch of oatmeal.

"Eat your oatmeal!" she'd tell me. "It'll stick to your ribs," my father would add. You bet! That obnoxious oatmeal stuck to everything — spoons, dishes, pots and pans. No wonder I won't touch oatmeal today!

Not that I'm against healthy foods. All I'm saying is that I'll leave oats to people who think oats comes from super-markets.

I have my own health food answer. In fact, I'll make a prediction. Grits! I predict grits will be the next wave of healthomania. I like grits.

Grits haven't caught on up here in Yankee-land yet. I predict they will. Eat grits I say, and you'll have true grit.

I first got acquainted with grits when I was in basic train-ing in Mississippi. Grits are the secret of the south's suc-cess. Ever notice the slow-paced life style down south? Grits! Up here it's Valium. Down there it's grits.

Momma and I took a trip to North Carolina awhile back. We pulled off the freeway for breakfast at a little out-of-the-way spot. The waitress came over, and we ordered up some ham and eggs.

Well, we waited. And we waited. Finally again the waitress came; and in her deep southern drawl said, "Ahm sorry, ya' all! But the cook had to go out for some more aigs!"

Grits! So what if the egg inventory was down. Go out and get a dozen. That's what I like about grits.

Somewhere right now hidden in the piney woods of Georgia, I say there's a secret laboratory. White-coated bearded scientists wearing thick glasses are busy taking grits apart.

And I'm predicting before long we'll hear that grits are good for everything that ails us.

And don't forget, you read it here first.

Making Hay

Making hay, my grandfathers always called it. "Gotta make hay when the sun shines!" they'd say to me, back more than fifty years ago.

And even today, one hears the expression. Not only at haying time, but when there's an important job of any kind that needs to get done.

Drive around the countryside these days, and you'll see the farmers hard at the task of putting up their winter's supply of alfalfa, clover and timothy — square bales, big round bales, and haylage, chopped hay that goes into silos.

Making hay's changed a lot since I first hooked my bare toes over the ladder of a farm wagon, guiding a team of hefty draft horses along windrows of freshly-cut, sweet-smelling clover.

The other afternoon, I was driving past Jeff Wilber's place, coming home from the tree farm. Jeff lives around the corner, first driveway to the right.

On his front lawn stands an antique hay mower, the kind my grandfathers used years ago. I'd eyed the ancient machine many times as I'd driven by. And finally, I couldn't resist the impulse to look at it closer; to touch it, to re-kindle memories of times long past.

"It's no doubt at least fifty years old," Jeff told me. "It's a Minnesota No. 3. I've restored it. Those are the original paint colors. Cost me $14.50 just for those little blades for the sickle bar."

"Jeff," I said, "see this scar on my forehead? That came when I was four years old. I fell off a mower just like this, and landed on the fly wheel! Took seven stitches to patch me up.

"I remember my grandfathers cutting hay with one of these," I continued. "I could hear them halfway across the farm as they drove their horses. 'Whoa! Back up! Now giddap!', they'd call."

Making hay, and all farming, has changed drastically since my boyhood. Then, it was horsepower. Now, it's still horsepower, but the kind that comes from beneath the hood of a big green-and-yellow John Deere.

Cut it any way you like though, and it's still hard work.

But I doubt it's as much fun — at least for a young boy. A week of putting up hay was an exciting, adventuresome week; time spent working side by side with grownups; effort that left me feeling important, contributing; a member of the team.

"Well, the hay's down," my grandfather would say, meaning he'd finished the cutting. "If it doesn't rain tonight, tomorrow I'll rake it." And the next day, I'd watch as Gramp made long windrows with his side-delivery rake, a wondrous machine that spun and swirled, spitting out an endless stream of timothy.

And a job for me. . .driving a team of horses that pulled a farm wagon, straddling the windrows. Trailing behind would be an old-fashioned hay loader, another wondrous machine, that conveyed the hay up over the rear of the wagon. Carefully, my Uncle Joe would stack the stuff, proud of his ability to build a big square load. Woe be it to anyone who had a corner of a load slip off on the way to the barn!

Onto the barn floor, the load would be driven.

Overhead, hanging from a steel track that ran the length of the barn, was another ingenious gadget, the hay cart; a miraculous machine fashioned of steel wheels and cogs.

From it, hung a big hay fork, two long tines of steel. Pulling on a rope, Uncle Joe would lower the hay fork, and ram it into the load. "Ready!" he'd holler.

Outside, stood Bobby, the oldest draft horse on the farm, patiently waiting for my Aunt Bernadette to lead him by his halter. On command, into his harness he'd lean, and the thick hay rope would speed through wooden pulleys, squeaking and groaning.

Up from the wagon, the huge bite of hay would rise to the roof of the barn. "Click!" the hay cart would echo, and, with a roar, disappear out of sight into the hay mow.

"Trip!" my Uncle Amy, up in the mow, would yell. And Uncle Joe would yank on his rope, releasing the hay for Amy to spread into the far corners of the mow with his three-tined pitch fork.

In short order, the wagon would be emptied. And back to the field, after a stop at the windmill for a vinegar jug of cold, sweet well water, capped with a corn cob, I'd go; a straw-hatted, bib-overalled, barefoot, young farm lad, driving his team of bays.

I was making hay — and good memories.

GRAND
CHAMPION

County Fairs

Well, county fair time is just around the corner.

Across the country, rural America will take a break. Farmers and city folk alike will take time to gather, to socialize a bit, to peer into a mirror called agriculture. And in that reflection, they'll see an image of what's going on in the nation's breadbasket.

County fairs are one of our finest institutions, I say. I went to my first a good fifty years ago, and during that interim, they've changed very little. And that's what I like about county fairs. With the pace of our lives accelerating every day, it's good to see something holding permanence and stability.

Sure, the tractors get bigger, and stock cars now race around blacktopped oval tracks where once the clippity-clop of horses' hoofs echoed on dirt and sand. But there's still the ferris wheel, spinning brightly in a full-mooned summer evening sky, and a merry-go-round, with excited, smiling kids perched on undulating red and gold miniature ponies.

And the crowd's the same, a good mix of small town folks out to look around, many savoring the roots of their own farm pasts, and country people musing on the fruits of their labors.

I've always found it easy to separate the two. Look for the sunbrowned arms and faces, foreheads lighter-toned, from being shielded by caps while working in the fields all day. They're the farm folks. Farm folks always stroll a little slower, more casually. They're tired. They've been working hard since sun-up. And they won't hang around until the last dog's hung. Tomorrow's another day, as they say, of getting the crops in.

City dwellers are more bouncy, wear shorts, and have to read the signs over in the poultry barn to tell a Rhode Island Red from a Leghorn.

Over the years, I've attended my share of county fairs. The scene hasn't changed much. Grown-ups still huddle in little knots, exchanging news of the day, to background music of the carousel's organ and the raucous chatter of sideshow barkers hustling their wares.

"Win a cupie doll for your girlfriend! Knock over the milk bottles and win a teddy bear for that little girl! Hey, there! How about some cotton candy?" the hustlers call.

Young boys rough-house each other along the midway. And pairs of teenagers walk hand-in-hand, first love in bloom. Babies still snooze peacefully in mothers' arms.

A banker, fancy dressed in shirt and tie, visits with an elderly farmer friend. The mortgage is paid off, and their interest now turns to the price of corn and soybean futures down in Chicago.

Through the crowd saunters a local politician, smiling, shaking hands, handing out "vote for me again" pamphlets, many of which end up underfoot in the trampled grass. There's a message. Taxes are too high.

Over in the livestock shed stand rows of prize-winning Guernseys and Holsteins. Overhead hang green-and-white clover-leafed 4-H Club and Future Farmers of America signs. Breaking the silence, a cow bellows loudly, probably announcing, "Enough of this stuff! Take me home to my comfortable stall in the barn."

A 4-H youngster moves about, lugging a pail of water and a pitchfork of hay to Old Bessie. Another carries a bucket of frothy milk, freshly hand-extracted from Maude.

Down the line, a trim young lady, dressed in faded blue jeans and red-and-white plaid blouse, busies herself curry-combing and brushing her blue-ribbon steer; a stocky, chunky animal that has T-bone steak written all over it.

I look into her face. It's solemn and serious. There's mixed emotion written there. Tomorrow Dandy Don will be in the auctioneer's ring, maybe bring the top dollar, money that will go toward the young lady's college education. Yet, she'd raised Dandy from a calf. And it's going to be hard to let go, to face the reality of being a farmer.

Across the way, in the homemaker's building, pairs and threesomes of middle-aged ladies pause to finger and admire crocheted afghans and needle-pointed pillows. "Now isn't that just beautiful!" they softly exclaim. Little boys impatiently tug at their hands, begging "Let's go, Mom!"

Outside, from beyond the grandstand, the first cannonlike "BOOM!" of fireworks echoes through the warm night.

It's county fair. . .Americana at its best!

A Family Reunion

"Roots. . . .roots". . . .I heard the words from an uncle, my sister, my cousin. You can find roots, you see, at family reunions.

Roots are substance — relatives to talk to, and old buildings to walk through. And roots are memories; ghost-like images that float before your eyes, of long-gone grandfathers and uncles striding across farm yards; of grandmothers and aunts leaning over silver-and-black wood-burning cookstoves.

The trip had been long, seven hours of fighting tailgating eighteen-wheelers and speedy sports cars on the interstate. I was tired. I'd had enough. And finally the turn onto the quiet, peaceful tree-lined country road.

The wonderful, old red-brick farm house came into view, and I eased into the driveway. A volleyball game was in progress on the front lawn, under the tall walnut and spruce trees. And my spirits began to soar. I was back to my roots. And I leaned on the car's horn. Hands waved back from kinfolk huddled, visiting, in a cluster of lawn chairs.

"Wie gehts!" my brother greeted me, extending his arm for a handshake. We're of German stock. And the old-country greeting still lingers in our clan. "How goes it?" is a fair English translation.

Roots lie in words, too.

My Uncle Vincent threw a great knuckle-ball. And he was in high demand fifty years ago as a local semi-pro baseball pitcher, for games played around the area on Sunday afternoons.

Come Sunday mornings, after church, he'd want to warm up his arm a bit. And he'd ask me to catch for him. So I'd grab the well-worn catcher's mitt, and out to the front lawn we'd go, right where the volleyball game was being played.

After a few easy lobs to loosen up his wing, he'd begin to bear down, throwing me that knuckle ball.

I was just a kid, maybe twelve, and toward me, dancing and bobbing through the air, would come that speeding knuckle ball pitch. Well, I'll tell you, it was a fearful thing — like trying to catch a butterfly with a teaspoon. Off my arms and chest, the ball would ricochet. It's a wonder I ended up with a tooth in my mouth!

Roots can be re-lived in emotions, too.

"Did I ever show you those old baseball pictures up in the attic?" Vince said to me.

"No," I answered. "I didn't even know about 'em." And up the stairs of the old house to the third floor we climbed. There at one end, pasted to the wall, was a collection of faded newspaper clippings, pictures of old-time baseball players. Two of Babe Ruth, others of Tris Speaker, Ty Cobb, Frankie Frisch, Bill Terry, and more. Treasures, if ever I've seen any.

"Vince," I said. "How old are these?"

"I suppose I put them there when I was about twelve. I'm 77 now, so that makes it about 65 years ago. Around 1925, I'd say. Baseball was a big thing with me back then."

"Thanks so much for showing them to me," I told him. And we turned to leave and rejoin the party.

And there stood my grandfather's old rocking chair, the one he sat in by the kitchen woodbox each night, smoking his corncob pipe, after the cows were milked.

Roots, in the far corners of an attic!

"You should have these," my Aunt Rita said, handing me an envelope. I opened it, and began to sift through its contents. An old photo of a great-grandfather, bearded, stern-faced. And an official looking document with an impressive seal at the bottom, dated December 5, 1884; his naturalization papers declaring him a citizen of the United States, and renouncing forever his allegience to the Emperor of Germany.

A second photo, of my great-grandmother, strength and resolve written in her face. Catherina was her name, one handed down many times through generations of descendants since. And a baptismal certificate, hand-written in Latin, dated April 4, 1857.

And old black-and-white snapshots of houses of the times, a barn with wood-staved silos, an old windmill, a lady dressed in long skirt and apron feeding her chickens.

They're mine now.

. . . . roots.

Ice Skating

Things were quiet, serene, peaceful — out there on the little lake. There I sat, resting on the seat of my ice fishing sled, jigging for walleyes through a hole in the ice, watching the inert flags of my tipups.

Dusk was falling.

To the west, behind a band of tall Norway pines, an anemic winter sun was settling, its last rays casting burnished silver, like that of polished pewter, on the snowless frozen surface of the lake. Over on the northeast shore where a summer cottage stands, the slanting sun beams reflected in brilliant gold from the dwelling's picture window.

Except for the distant whine of a chainsaw and the raucous crowing of a pair of crows heading for their night's roosting, all was still; almost a classic December 'silent night' in northern Wisconsin.

The scene could have been right out of an old Currier and Ives painting. You know, one of those old-fashioned winter portraits. Yet inside me, an unsettling instinct stirred, telling me something was amiss. What? For several fleeting moments the question gnawed at me. And then the answer dawned.

Ice skaters! That's what was missing! A young couple dressed in baggy wools of the 1920's, long red and green scarfs trailing behind in the breeze, gliding gracefully over the lake. That's what the picture needed!

And old, long-muted memories began to replay in my brain. Ice skating, you see, was a big thing for my generation of youngsters.

This past summer, a brother and I got to reminiscing about our lives as kids back in the late 1930's. "I remember getting a pair of skates for Christmas," Bill told. "I tried them on to make sure they were big enough. And believe me, they were! A couple sizes oversize! So I'd have room to grow into them! Mom made sure of that!"

Experiences like that well typify those times. Money was scarce, people were poor. And we youngsters found our recreation in simple ways, like sledding on Deak's Hill, or skating on the pond across the road.

The little puddle wasn't all that much, maybe a half acre in size, surrounded by big oaks fringing a farm field. There after supper, we'd gather. Approach the site; and the voices of friends, boys and girls, would grow from a distant murmur in the night air to the excited clamor of country kids having fun.

Kids of all ages and backgrounds. The more well-to-do apparent by the pairs of "shoe" skates hanging from laces around their necks. The less-well-off obvious by the old-fashioned "clamp" skates they carried.

Clamp skates were made to be fastened to the soles of your shoes. With a key, the blades would be tightened in place. In theory, the clamps were supposed to hold. But in reality, they frequently twisted loose, sending frustrated skaters spilling to the ice. And pity the youngster, who tore the sole from his shoe in the process. For shoes were precious, and a scolding was inevitable when the unfortunate one got home.

If the night's cold warranted, wood was gathered, and a fire built. And in its dim light, makeshift hockey games would organize. No store-bought hockey sticks like now-days. Just sturdy crooked sticks cut from bushes and trees. And the pucks, just a gnarled knot to be batted around until finally splitting into pieces. The older, bigger guys, the better and faster skaters, usually played hockey.

The rest of the gang was content to casually skate slowly in circles around the perimeter of the pond, laughing, teasing; with a periodic game of "crack the whip" sending a brave skater sailing at what seemed breathtaking speed across the ice.

For many years now, the little pond has been gone, filled and killed by a housing development that came in the boom that followed World War II. Yet I know where its waters once stood. And when I visit my home turf, especially in winter, I gaze across the rows of modern homes.

There, marked by a few aged sturdy oaks that still remain, my memory once more paints for me images of youngsters happily skating on moonlit winter evenings.

For the fun of it.

Christmas in a Country School

Christmases in one-room country schools many years ago — what were they like? Talk to Ida Shoquist. She can tell you.

I'd heard about the old time, long-gone school from a neighbor, Jeff Wilber. Jeff lives around the corner from my Christmas tree farm. "It was called the Oak Hill school," he said. "You oughta visit with my grandmother. She could tell you all about it."

And his words led me recently to Ida Shoquist, a chipper 84-year-old; grandmother to 19, great-grandmother to 21. In the home where she's lived since 1929, when she and Ray, her late husband, first began farming; I listened, fascinated, as Ida told me her story.

"My folks came here in 1898 by covered wagon from Indiana," she said. "My dad gave the land, one acre, to the school district for the Oak Hill school. It was built in 1905 on a hilltop at the crossroads just east of your place. The countryside was heavily wooded with oak trees at that time. So that's how it got its name."

What was the country like back then, I asked.

"There wasn't too much farmland then, just ten-acre clearings here and there. And the roads were just wagon trails through the woods, very rough" she replied.

And the school?

"It was very small," she continued, "maybe thirty feet

by fifty. It was painted yellow and had a little entryway. On the north and south walls were large windows, to allow light for reading. There was a big pot-bellied stove, and neighborhood menfolks would cut loads of wood for heat. We had kerosene lamps, but most of our studying was done by daylight. No well — we had to carry our drinking water. And we carried our lunches, in syrup pails."

Ida began first grade at Oak Hill in 1912. "There were about 24 students in grades one through eight," she told. "We studied reading, writing, and arithmetic. We had a big blackboard, and we used slates to write on. We learned a lot of poetry. I loved that the best! I'm still very much interested in poetry."

"The teacher called us to class by ringing a hand bell. Our teachers had it rough," she added. "They walked a long ways from where they boarded. In the winter they had to build the fires. And all for maybe thirty dollars a month!"

How did the kids dress, I inquired.

"There were no snowsuits in those days," she smiled. "The boys wore overalls; the girls long underwear, stockings and long dresses. We didn't know what slacks were. In the winter, the roads weren't plowed. I remember wearing two-buckle overshoes."

"Almost all of our clothing was handmade. I don't think I ever had a store-bought dress. Mittens and socks were hand-knit of wool."

And Christmases — how did you celebrate Christmas, I asked.

"Well, the school was always quite cold. It seemed like the winters were always bad back then. But we always had nice Christmas programs. People walked or travelled by horse and wagon, or sleighs. They didn't have much money. Folks dressed the best they could. It was about the only time of year a girl got a new dress.''

In advance of the big day, boys from the school would go out into the woods to cut a Christmas tree. ''The teacher would help us trim it. We had some ornaments but no lights like today. We used candleholders and real candles. There was a danger of fire; but people were careful, and nothing got burnt.''

''Parents and families came, and we spoke pieces and sang carols. Santa came, and we exchanged gifts. We'd draw names ahead for a gift to a classmate. It wasn't much, just some little thing. And we had apples and popcorn balls for treats. Those programs in the evenings by kerosene lamplight bring back a lot of memories.''

Today, the school site is occupied by a private home. Drive by, and you'll see no trace of the simple one-room frame building where attentive country youngsters once received their educations in the three R's.

Except me. I'm one of the fortunates. Because now as I pass to tend my Christmas tree flock, I can pause there — on the hill, at that corner. And I can allow my imagination a full, free rein.

There, thanks to a neighborly great-grandmother, I'll see horse-drawn sleighs parked on snowy nights, the flicker of a kerosene lamp through single-pane windows. And I'll hear the nervous voice of a youngster saying his piece, the notes of *Silent Night* and *O' Little Town of Bethlehem*.

Especially this time of year.

At Christmas.

Of Firewood and Oil

"Making wood" my grandfathers always called it. Making wood was the winter job of putting up firewood. And now, almost sixty years later, I find myself still at it.

Just recently I bought a truckload of oak pulpwood, ten cords, which I'm in the process of reducing to firewood. A lot of people get their firewood that way.

Like those folks, we heat almost exclusively with wood, going back to 1980 when I'd gotten puckered by a so-called energy crisis. On an early November day that year, as Ronald Reagan was being elected president, a heating contractor came to install a wood burning attachment onto our oil furnace.

"Connie," we've come to call the converter unit, a loyal and faithful servant if there ever was one. True, she's a demanding lady. There's no such thing as a free lunch when you heat with wood. Chimneys need cleaning and ashes need hauling. And above all, the midnight feedings; trips to the basement to re-stoke her tummy, to keep her happy and purring.

So the big truck and trailer came the other day. Al Voight, the driver, had a heck of a time jockeying his rig around some of the tight corners out at the tree farm where I wanted the wood stacked. But he finally made it, being the expert he is at maneuvering his fifty-foot rig into tight places.

And now, when the mood strikes, there I find myself, armed with chainsaws and splitting maul, reducing the long logs to short logs. It's a job I don't dislike. Some may say it's a lot of hard work. And that's true. But it's good hard work, the kind that loosens up the vertebrae and flattens the gut muscles. And at the end of the day, you've got something to show for your efforts, a nice pile of freshly split, pungent smelling firewood.

There's more. Work alone all day and a person gets to do considerable thinking. So with me. And I get to pondering imponderable subjects — like oil; how oil has affected our lives. Like how we've moved from an almost oil-less society back in my grandfathers' days, to one totally dominated by and dependent on the stuff today.

There I work, swinging my roaring chainsaw, which is powered by gasoline made from oil. The firewood I'm manufacturing, I'll haul home with the nearby pickup, also powered by oil, to replace oil to heat the house.

Not like grandpa's days, I say. And my memory wanders back to long ago times when I'd traipse along behind my uncles on gray, snowy mornings to the family woodlot. No four-wheel drive pickups to bust through the snowdrifts. We walked, single file, beating down the trail with overshoed boots.

Over the shoulder of an uncle, hung a cross-cut saw, undulating up and down as he walked, a tool fueled by muscle power, not liquid from a long-nozzled red can.

Pulling a cross-cut saw all day was hard work. Yet crosscuts had advantages. For one thing, they always started, even on the coldest mornings. No messing with spark plugs or carburetors.

And cross-cuts were quiet. You didn't need ear muffs to save your hearing. The only sound one heard was the 'swish-swish-swish', as the six-foot band of steel bit into the log, spitting streams of yellow sawdust with each stroke. Unless of course, you weren't doing your share of the work, like riding the saw. Then your partner might say something, maybe something not so nice. And you'd hear him, that's for sure!

When the job was done, the logs cut, horsepower was used to move them. Real horsepower. . .a team of broad-shouldered bays fueled by hay and oats, not diesel fuel. Along the lane from the woods to the barnyard, a bobsled — not a huge logging truck — would move, carrying the wood.

There, behind the big red brick farmhouse, stood Gramp's one concession to oil, his Model 10-20 McCormick Deering tractor, powering the saw rig that buzzed the logs into firewood.

In the sixty-years that have passed, our society has moved from almost an oil-less culture into one that's oil-addicted. Today, we exist as we do because of oil.

As I write this, another president struggles with an international crisis revolving around oil. I find myself pondering how many similar crises civilization will face in the future.

By the time these words reach print, the bombs may be falling, the bullets flying.

And I agonize.

Country Store

A business carved from the backwoods wilderness. . . that's what I'd call it. One of those mom-and-pop type enterprises that once dotted our north country, now fast disappearing in the face of modern-day economic pressures.

The two-storied yellow frame building rests comfortably alongside the county highway in northwestern Washburn County, nestled on a pie-shaped piece of land between the road and the pretty little lake that ripples in the sun at its back door.

For over half a century, the combination general store, gas station, and tavern has been there; a landmark in the area, serving local residents and passersby. High above its front door hangs a white sign, its fading red letters announcing simply, "Mac Lake Store."

And therein, is represented an era; that of Blanche and Glen Grimes. For they operated that business since the early 1940's. Glen is gone now, passing on in 1987. And Blanche, now 84, resides upstairs over the once bustling general store.

I visited with Blanche recently. A mutual acquaintance had suggested that I do so. "She's a delightful person," my friend had said, an assessment that couldn't have been more accurate.

"Glen and I came here in 1941," Blanche told. "The

store was already here, but three people had gone broke running it. And a lot of folks said we would too. Times were very hard. But we thought there was a demand for food, and it worked out.''

The store served a large area, with other stores located in distant communities like Trego, Spooner and Minong.

"The county highway was just a dirt road back then.'' she said. "In the summer, the dust was terrible. And snow removal in the winter was unheard of.''

The Grimes' also had three log cabins on their property, which they rented to tourists, primarily from Indiana and Illinois, in the summer. Some came by train.

"There was no electricity,'' she recalled. "We did have a generator for lights in the store and tavern, but that was all. The cabins had woodstoves, iceboxes, kerosene lamps, and outside toilets. People came for a week or two on vacations to swim and fish. Mac Lake had a reputation for good-sized bass, panfish and northern pike. Glen caught a twenty pound northern from it one winter.''

Without electricity, refrigeration was a problem.

"In the winter we'd cut ice from the lake,'' she continued. "That was our winter carnival. We'd put it up in an ice house, and that's what we used to cool our beer and pop all summer.''

While Glen ran the tavern, Blanche took care of the store.

"We sold everything from rifle shells to shoe laces,'' she said. "We bought meat from the local farmers, and sold steak for a few cents a pound. But without refrigeration, people preferred wieners and baloney that had preservatives. I canned a lot of fresh meat that we didn't sell.''

"I remember when we sold eggs for seven cents a dozen,'' she added. "And our vinegar came in kegs, apples and oranges by the bushel, and bananas by the stalk.

Everything had to be weighed and packaged."

On Saturday nights, the tavern adjoining the store would come alive with social activity.

"Glen would hire a band and hold dances," Blanche reminisced. "The place would be so packed that the customers would have to stand outside while people danced inside. Everybody had a good time. And in all the years we were here, we never had to call the law."

"While their folks socialized, I'd babysit the kids. Those kids are coming back now. And they tell me how they remember the big ice cream cones I'd fix for them."

Back in those old days, business was often done on credit, Blanche said.

"Once we had over $5,000 out on account. Glen composed a letter and sent it to our customers. Out of all of them, only one didn't pay his bill. Some took two years! I thought that was pretty wonderful."

Blanche showed me around the old store the other day. Its shelves and showcases now stand empty. The old oak desk, where she spent many hours keeping the books, rests idle, its rolltop closed.

"I ran the store until I was eighty," she said, pausing. "Then I closed it, and leased the tavern."

"My son and daughter-in-law want me to come to Illinois to live with them. But I don't want to leave."

And I understood why.

Good memories are hard to move.

Farm Breakfasts

Dead-winter mornings are dark, dreary things. I awaken, and outside the world is black. Daylight arrives slowly in mid-winter.

I sip my first cup of coffee, read the morning paper, and still the backyard remains cloaked in gloom. And as breakfast, a batch of Malt-O-Meal, simmers on the kitchen range, my thoughts drift back to mornings long ago; back to my boyhood. . .back to breakfasts on farms many years ago.

The bubbling cereal triggers my reminiscing. A hot cereal! Everyone I knew as a boy. . .my folks, my grandparents, my uncles and aunts. . .all would say that a bowl of hot cereal, either oatmeal or cornmeal, was the best way for a youngster to start the day. Especially when there was a mile-walk through the cold and snow to a country school.

I can hear my grandfather now. "Eat it!" he'd say, as I'd wrinkle my nose at the glue-like oatmeal before me, so thick it'd have to be scraped from the serving spoon. "It's good for you," he'd say. "It'll stick to your ribs!" Which meant it had staying power. Which it did. Which is why I hate oatmeal to this day.

I look around our kitchen as I eat, at the array of push-button gadgets that instantaneously respond to our commands; the electric range, the coffe-maker, the toaster, the micro-wave, the lights that illuminate the house.

And I think about similar dark, dead-winter mornings, back when my grandfather started each day by banging an old wrench on the cast-iron radiator in his bedroom. The clanging carried along the pipes to the upstairs bedrooms where he six sons and three daughters slept. Time to roll out! Cows needed milking, horses needed feeding, the sound said.

By the time "The Boys", as grandpa fondly referred to his sons, came marching down the stairs, grandma would already be busy in her kitchen, building a fire in her wood-burning range. Breakfast had to be prepared for the gang. In an hour or so, the men would be back from their barn chores. And they'd be hungry.

Quickly, silently, the menfolks slipped into their barn clothing, heavy denim coats and four-buckle overshoes. In the entryway, kerosene lanterns would be lighted, shiny milk pails selected. Down the back porch steps into the darkness they slipped, the swinging lanterns casting ghostly shadows with their pale yellow light; past the big wood pile and the windmill, the snow creaking and crunching under their booted feet. And into the barn they'd disappear, to where the herd of Holsteins and Guernseys patiently waited in their stanchions.

I suppose the milking, the feeding and watering of the livestock would take a strong hour of their time. When finished, back to the house they'd drift. . .for breakfast.

And what breakfasts they would be! Grandma and her daughter helpers, my aunts, would have been busy; the long oil-cloth covered table set, the food simmering on her wood stove.

Grandpa always sat at the head of the table; the boys along his right, the girls along his left. Grandma at the op-posite end, when she had a chance to sit, that is.

From her oven, placed there to be kept hot, would come huge platters of eggs, fried in bacon grease. No, you didn't get a choice as to how you'd like yours done. Alongside were heaping mounds of bacon and pork sausage, made from hogs raised on the farm and butchered the previous fall.

Then a steaming platter of warmed-over potatoes, homegrown too, deliberately left from supper the night before.

Loaves of golden brown bread, baked, perhaps the day before, in the very same oven; cut into thick slices, ready for the butter she'd churned or the plum jam she'd canned last summer.

And the best of all! Her buckwheat pancakes! Massive things that covered an entire plate, to be topped with sweet apple butter made from the Yellow Transparents that grew in her orchard. Pancakes made from flour ground at the mill in town, of grain that grandpa grew in the little patch of buckwheat he planted each spring.

As appetites were staved, spirits improved. Jovial talk rolled around the table. And grandpa would get in his licks as to what he expected his crew to accomplish that day. Things like pulling a crosscut saw in the woods cutting firewood, or fanning seed oats in the granary for spring planting.

I look back at those long-ago breakfasts with mixed feelings. Certainly they were wonderful family times. Yet, I find myself amazed at how those old-timers did it, especially my grandmother. Seven days a week, most of her life, she made those breakfasts.

And when we'd get up from her table to resume our days, it'd still be dark outside.

Farming's Changed

"Farming's sure changed," I remarked, my foot resting on the wheel of the old corn cultivator.

"It sure has!" Roy Spexet responded. "A farmer today wouldn't even look at this stuff!" The two of us were standing amidst an array of antique farm implements that Spexet has collected, and is in the process of restoring.

"It's just a hobby," Roy said. "I got started about three years ago when I retired. I bought a team of draft horses then, and I got interested in the equipment that went with them. Most of the pieces I found at auction sales."

Spexet is no stranger to old horse-drawn farm machinery. His folks had a farm on the south end of Potato Lake east of Spooner. And there, as a youth, he learned to handle horses and to operate the farm equipment of the times.

"Bet you've never seen one of these," he said, pointing to an ancient plow. "It's a breaking plow and was used to break new ground for cultivation."

The old utensil had history written all over it — on its weatherbeaten oak beam, the curved wooden handles. "It's even got a wooden wheel up front. That regulated the depth of the furrow," he said. Made prior to 1900, the unit has been beautifully restored in red and silver.

And we moved to a second machine; sturdy, solid, of steel construction. "This is a horse-drawn grader. It's called 'The Roadster', and it was made in 1909 in Minneapolis by the Russell Grader Manufacturing Company. Years ago, all our roads were patrolled with horse-drawn graders.''

Next, an old manure spreader, refurbished in green and yellow. Horse-drawn also, it's a miniature, scaled-down version of the power operated units seen today being pulled by big tractors. "It's pretty much original," Roy said, "only the seat's missing."

As we strolled amongst the old machines, thoughts of my own boyhood came sifting back. The scene stirred fond memories of my grandfathers and their farmyards of the 1930's.

"This is an International horse-drawn side delivery rake," Roy said. "It could operate both forward and in reverse. Forward it raked the hay. Backward, it flipped the hay in the air to dry it."

And on to an old dump hay rake. "I remember my grandfather operating one of these," I said. "He always used his youngest team so he could race them across the cut field."

Past an old two-horse tumble bucket scraper, wagons, an aged mower with its rusty oil can still in place, walking plows, a bobsled with wooden runners, an old feed grinder, a grain drill, and an Aspinwall-Watson potato planter made in Houlton, Maine.

Some of the old machines had grease cups. And therein lies a page of our country's industrial history. "We went from the oil can for lubricating, to the grease cup, to the Zerk fitting and the grease gun," Roy noted.

Then a look into the shop where he does his repair work. "I make my own singletrees, eveners, and neck yokes. I've got two sawmills out back where I saw my own lumber. And I make my own poles, all out of oak."

And finally, a chance to meet up with Jim and Dan, his team of Belgian-breed draft horses. Beautiful animals, it'd been a long time since I'd patted the forehead of a work horse.

"They're five and six years old, respectively," Spexet said. "They'll go about 2,300 pounds. I use them to pull the implements. I had them out plowing the other day." Later, Mary, his wife said that people had stopped their cars on the highway that day to take pictures of Roy and the horses.

Spexet's nostalgic love for his horses and machinery shows. "You can take the horses out and it's so peaceful. No noise, just the clink-clink of chains. And you don't have to spend a couple dollars for gas just to start the engine," he says.

And his goal? "I'd like to get a complete line set up for people to come and look at," he told me. "I'd like to see some of the old machines preserved, maybe in a farm museum. I wonder if there's going to be such a place where our great grandchildren can look at this old equipment. Are they going to know what it looked like?"

"Our young people today are losing touch with the dirt, the soil!" he commented.

Roots, I call it, Roy. Roots!

And you are so right.

Lumberjacks

Logging camps...river drives...narrow gauge railroads... all pages in the history of our forests here in northern Wisconsin.

A little magazine came in the mail the other day; my copy of *"Chips and Sawdust,"* a publication put out by the Forest History Association of Wisconsin. The group is comprised of people in the forestry, logging, and timber manufacturing fields; folks who are dedicated to preserving some of our colorful lumbering past, an era that goes back to the virgin timber days at the turn of the century.

It's an effort that I applaud.

For the words that appear each week in this column are written in a mini-forest history atmosphere; here in my basement "wreck" room, which I decided years ago would have an old logging camp decor — rough-sawn hemlock panelling on the walls and time-worn crosscut saws, cant hooks, peavies, and double-bitted axes hanging there from.

Not that I'm an authority on Wisconsin forest history. But with almost forty years of ramming around in the far corners of our backwoods, I've had fair opportunity to see some of the remains of the early logging days. The traces are there if you have an eye for them, written on the land in old railroad grades, splash dams and camp sites.

But time is slowly taking its toll on the old evidence.

Back in the 1950's, when most of my workdays were spent in the woods, cruising and mapping timber, recognizing the old relics was relatively easy. And I came upon many long-abandoned logging campsites. What a thrill it was to poke around in the ruins and ponder how the lumberjacks lived and worked in those places.

And, over time, I've had the pleasure of meeting and getting to know some of those old-time lumberjacks. Nels Olson of Mason, for example. In his book, *"Time in Many Places,"* Olson describes in authentic detail, life in the old camps and sawmills where he worked as a young man.

Another lumberjack who turned author was George Corrigan of Saxon who, in his book *"Calked Boots and Cant Hooks,"* tells of the early-century logging days in the Mellen area. Long ago, I once had the privilege of spending a day in the woods with George. And later, we corresponded about a second book he was contemplating.

Then a lumberjill, Esther Gibbs, of Spooner. Esther also wrote a book, *"We Went A Loggin'."* And in it, she tells of times after World War I when she and her husband worked as cooks for a large logging camp in the Chippewa River country south of Ladysmith. Her accounts of camp life are some of the most descriptive I've read.

There were others, men who didn't write books, but still could tell the stories. Like Leo Gould, the old forest ranger at Tomahawk, who told me about log drives on the Prairie River into Merrill. How, on the spring mornings, the jacks would be a bit slow getting into the cold water. And how the boss in his thick Irish brogue would yell, "Get in there! It won't bu-r-r-rn ya!"

And some of the old-timers I worked with in the 60's on the Menominee Indian forest east of Antigo! Like Alex Waupoose. Alex was the logging superintendent, responsible for all the cutting in the woods. He and I worked closely. A wonderful gentlemen, I enjoyed his accounts of the old days.

Then Bogue Dickie, a Menominee logger. I got to know Bogue well on my visits to his jobs. And I cherish the moments we spent together, sitting on big yellow birch logs, visiting. He'd tell about the old camps; of the narrow-gauge railroads that hauled the logs before trucks came to the woods. Of the log drives down the Wolf and Oconto rivers that he took part in, and the dangerous log jams he witnessed.

There's a homemade coffee table here, standing nearby as I write. It's one I made many years ago from an ancient rusty circular saw, a blade that came from an old sawmill. Gordon Fleming, a logger I knew in the 50's over at Park Falls, gave it to me.

The old saw reposes quietly now. Yet, I find myself looking at it and wondering how many big white pine logs it sawed into lumber, how many long-gone woodsmen listened to its whine.

It's a genuine piece of Wisconsin's forest history, a gift from a genuine Wisconsin lumberjack.

Birchwood Postmaster

To our friends up the street, Bill and Nancy Lindenberger, she's "Aunt Irene."

"You really oughta meet Aunt Irene," they'd said one day recently. "She's got some good stories about the old days in Birchwood when she ran the post office there."

Now, I like tales of the past — nostalgia, especially when it comes first-hand from people who've lived it. And so a recent day, Momma and I paid a visit to Irene Knapmiller, "Aunt Irene", as I too have come to know her; at the convalescent home in Rice Lake where she now spends her days.

The chipper, feisty 89-year-old was waiting to greet us, little notepad in hand listing carefully jotted items she'd chosen to talk about. No sooner had we gotten to know each other, when Bud, her son, and his wife Ruth arrived; up from their home in Cedarburg to visit also. And for a long hour, we four listened, enthralled with the lady's stories of her past.

"My dad was a newspaperman in Antioch, Illinois," Irene told. "But he decided to quit that and come north to farm. I graduated as a teacher from the Barron County Normal School at Rice Lake in 1920. I taught in one-room country schools at Barronett, Pokegema Prairie east of Cameron, Turtle Lake and Angus."

"But in the late 1920's, I moved to Birchwood, and got

married. When the postmaster job opened up, I went after it," she said. "I was appointed acting postmaster by President Franklin D. Roosevelt in 1934. And I served for 38 years, until I retired in 1972."

Aunt Irene went on to tell how the mail moved in those times.

"The old Tuscobia railroad line ran from Rice Lake to Park Falls, through Birchwood. The trains hauled logs, but they all had mail cars," she recalled. "Deliveries on the two Star Routes were by horses and canvas-covered wagons. Later, cars or trucks were used, but in winter the snow stopped them. Sometimes the mail wouldn't get through for days."

"And in the spring, the roads would be full of mud and sinkholes. Farmers would come with horses to pull the carriers out."

Irene vividly recalls the winter night in 1944, when fire swept through the business section of Birchwood, destroying an entire block, including the post office.

"The lumber mill was shut down," she said. "But they kept steam up. At one o'clock in the morning the mill whistle blew, and I got up to see where the fire was. It was forty below out."

"At the time, the post office was part of the LaPointe and Cyr Store, a general store that sold everything. We could see the fire coming, and I and the carriers moved the mail, desks and furniture across the street to the village hall. Two cases of money orders were stored in one of my upstairs bedrooms for safekeeping."

For the next twenty years, the post office was located in Harry LaPointe's store. Then, in 1964, Irene and her husband, Elmer, had a brick building built, which has served as the post office to this day.

Life as a small-town postmaster was interesting, Irene

says. "People are fussy about their mail. You meet all kinds — rich, poor, millionaires and multi-millionaires. Some nice and some not so nice."

She recalls the World War II times. "I was the government's agent in the area. When a serviceman was killed or missing in action. I got the word and had to deliver the message to his kin. I had three such missions to carry out."

"Once two women came to the post office to protest against the war and the government. I almost threw them out bodily. I told them, 'you're not going to talk against the government to me! There's the door!' "

More pleasantly, she remembers the cartons of baby chickens that would arrive every spring. "People ordered chicks, and they'd come by mail. The post office would be filled with their cheeping."

"Then the Bohemian people in the area would pick mushrooms and ship big bags of them back to Chicago. And Indian people would bring ginseng roots in for shipping."

And Irene has a fond place in her heart for the mail service she helped to provide. "All the trains had mail clerks who sorted the mail enroute. We could send a letter out of Birchwood by train at night, and have it delivered in Chicago the next day. You can't do that today!

"It was a great life!" she reminisced. "I liked it."

. . .And her face lights up at the memories.

Straw Hats

I bought a new straw hat the other day. So that's newsworthy, you say?

It is to me.

Straw hats and I, you see, go back a long time together. Back to days, as a boy, when the donning of a new straw hat was a ritual, a rite that took place shortly after my country one-room school closed for the summer, when my tattered baseball cap would become too warm for wear around the farm.

"Bring the boys some straw hats home from the store," my mother would call to my dad as he cranked up his trusty Model A Ford for a trip to town. And for something like fifteen cents each, my brothers and I would find ourselves equipped with new straw hats. . .like all the other farm kids in the neighborhood.

For the months of summer, except for church on Sundays, the new lids would be our constant companions as we drove horses on hay wagons, shocked grain bundles, and brought the cows home for milking from grandpa's woods.

It's easy to see why straw hats and I have a deep affection for each other.

So the other day, as I was walking along main street, I came upon a display of straw hats stacked on a table in front of Gordon Regenauer's little store. Maybe I should get one, I thought.

After all, the one back in the pickup was getting pretty ragged, what with Butch, my dog, sitting on it every now and then, cracking and breaking the green celluloid sun screen on its visor; like, perhaps, I'd walked into a popple tree out at my Christmas tree plantation.

And up at its crown, there's a big hole where the straw sticks out, all frazzled, in every direction; like, perhaps, a horse took a bite out of it. Through that hole, the deerflies and mosquitoes fly, to buzz around inside before settling on my bald spot. By chance, if I happen to be humming a little tune while they're doing their buzzing, the sound is not unlike that of an old time radio station.

Anyway, Gordie didn't have my size. "Tell those people who make these hats down in Mexico, that we have some big-headed Germans up here!" I told him. And down the street to Leo Root's Outlet Store, I went.

There, piled neatly on a counter, I found what I was looking for. . .a nice selection of straw hats; the cowboy variety, plain-and-simple farmer models, dressy brands, ladies' for working in their gardens, and cute kids' styles with drawstrings to tuck under little chins. And some in my size!

I looked the array over, trying to decide which suited me the best. And old memories of my uncles came floating back. Like visions from the past, there they stood... freshly-washed bib overalls, blue denim shirts with the sleeves rolled up over their muscled, sun-browned arms. And on their heads, straw hats!

My uncles always wore their straw hats with style. Maybe they spent a buck or two more, getting the better-made models. Anyway, their hats always had class. . .brims that had a trim, neat roll to them, hats that had a daring, jaunty air about them.

There, staring me in the face on Leo's counter, was one of those daring, jaunty jobs; a hat with character in its neat curvy visor and fancy blue-and-yellow plaid band. And in my size!

What the heck! Live it up! Get something daring and jaunty for a change! Something that'll look good at the county fair, yet still not too bold for shearing those Christmas trees, I said. So I bought it!

It's a hat like my uncles wore as they put up hay and cultivated corn many years ago, a hat that was the trademark of long-ago farmers.

Several years ago I wrote a column about red bandana handkerchiefs. In it, I said that the red bandana, along with the long-handled shovel and the double-bitted axe, should be placed on display at the Smithsonian Institute down at Washington D.C.. . .to commemorate the generations of sweat and toil that built this country.

Add a straw hat to that.

The Movies

Movies; Momma and I went to one the other night. It's rare when we go to one any more. My feeble mind, it seems, can't handle the stuff that most are made of these days.

But *"Field of Dreams"* was on.

"You'll like it," Momma said. After 39 years of marriage, she knows me pretty well.

There we sat in the half-darkness, the red "Exit" signs glowing, listening to the muffled talk of others around us, waiting for the show to start.

"Will this thing be in Technicolor?" I asked, still not sure I wanted to be there. She burst into a laugh and said, "I'm going to pretend I didn't hear that!"

And it dawned on me how dumb the question had sounded, how it had labelled me, how it had demonstrated how out of touch I was with the movie times. And I did some thinking, reflecting back on years past when going to a movie on a Sunday afternoon was a big thing for a youngster. And later, in teenage years, what a heady feeling it was to take a best girl to one.

The country's changed, of course. And so have we, the people. Simple pleasures, like two dollars spent on a couple movie tickets topped off with malted milks at the corner ice cream parlor, don't cut it anymore. Today it's — well, I don't have to tell you. You know. And I don't know if it's for the better or the worse.

Erma Bombeck, a nationally syndicated columnist, one I read regularly, wrote recently about how she longs for what she calls "a touch of elegance" once again in the world. Amen, Erma! We certainly could use a tad more taste and class. I applaud.

For that's how I remember the movies of thirty , forty years ago. Maybe they were a bit on the fantasy side. Maybe they did paint an unrealistic picture of life, what with the good guys always coming out on top. But they did have a touch of elegance.

Get Gene Kelly, Fred Astaire, Ginger Rogers, or Judy Garland up there singing and dancing with a big band playing in the background, and you had elegance.

And when "The End" flashed on the screen, you were sorry, reluctant to leave; yet happy, feeling good; glad that for an hour or two, life had been brighter.

There's no doubt in my mind, that movies played a tremendous role in maintaining the morale of the country during the World War II years. The nation was locked in a desperate life and death struggle. In the Pacific, the Japanese were kicking us around. Europe had been overrun by the Nazis. And at home, fathers and mothers were kissing eighteen-year-old sons goodbye, not knowing when or if they'd ever seen them again. Many didn't.

The country needed uplifting, and the movie people did a job. Hollywood came through, providing entertainment and diversion, psychic nourishment that boosted spirits, making the sacrifices and burdens a little more bearable.

Young and old went to the movies. My hometown, not large by any means, had five movie theaters. And they were always packed to the point where one worried about getting a seat. Double features! Three hours of Betty Grable, Alice Faye and Paulette Goddard. And Jeanne

Crain! How I drooled over Jeanne Crain in *"Margie"* and *"County Fair."*

The lights finally dimmed the other night, and I settled back. First, the coming attractions. Just like the old days, I thought. And I found myself looking forward to the newsreel. Every old movie house had a newsreel.

But no, not any more. No more Movietone News with Lowell Thomas' clear, crisp voice narrating a volcano erupting in the Fiji Islands or mountain climbing in the Himalayas.

Well, maybe the cartoon. I always liked the cartoons. Porky Pig, Daffy Duck, or Woody Woodpecker, my favorite. No, no cartoon either. So I'm getting old, I figure.

But then, the main feature, *"Field of Dreams,"* comes on. And in Technicolor yet!

Set in the farm country of Iowa, the story's about a young farmer so obsessed with a dream, that he plows under his corn crop to build a baseball diamond; a place where old-time major leaguers, idols of his youth, are reincarnated to come to play.

There's a moral, too, to the movie. Dream long enough, hard enough in life, and even the impossible can become possible.

Momma said I'd like the show. She was right.

It had a touch of class, you see.

Snowstorms

Bertha Falk was a neighbor of ours. A spinster, she and her bachelor brother ran a small farm a quarter-mile or so down the road from our place.

My mother had sent me on an errand to Bertha's. Maybe ten years old, I trudged through the deep snowdrifts that blocked our narrow town road, snow leaking down the tops of my four-buckle overshoes. Outlined in the snow that covered the roadside fields, I could see the trail neighborhood farmers had made with their teams of horses and bobsleds, as they struggled each morning to get their milk to market.

The time was the mid-1930's, a period marked by severe winters. And the scene, my first recollection of a major snowstorm, has remained etched in my mind to this day.

Live in Wisconsin, and one had better accept winter as a harsh reality. Since Halloween, my yard has looked like the North Pole. Any day, I expect a polar bear to come galloping across the snowdrifts with an Eskimo in hot pursuit.

But it's hard to find anything funny about a snowstorm. Roads get slippery, accidents occur, people get hurt. Electrical power fails, furnaces don't run, farmers can't get their cows milked.

Yet, some twenty-plus years ago, in the late 60's, I recall a snowstorm that had a humorous side to it.

I, and four other men, had been assigned to attend a forestry conference at Columbus, Ohio. In late October, the three-day affair looked like a piece of cake, the weather typically autumnal, brisk and sunny, as we'd driven down.

But by the close of the third day, as we prepared to leave for home, the weather reports turned ominous. An early season snowstorm was sneaking into the midwest, they said.

Yet, as we rolled westward out of Columbus on Interstate 70, we were in a jovial mood. We'd make Indianapolis, we figured, and there, hole up for the night.

Little did we know!

As late afternoon turned to darkness, snowflakes began to spit against our windshield, lightly at first, then thickening into a curtain of white. Traffic; cars, and trucks of all sizes, slowed to a crawl as the highway slickened. And the first casualties of the storm, cars down embankments and eighteen-wheelers jackknifed in the median, began to appear. The situation had grown deadly serious.

Slowly we limped along, and with midnight approaching, an exit sign for Richmond, Indiana appeared in the swirling whiteness. Choosing discretion over valor, onto the ramp we drove, looking for a place to eat and sleep.

Richmond was jammed with travelers with the same objectives, we soon learned. Motels were hopeless. But we located a nice supper club. At least, we'd get some food.

Inside, as we ordered, the manager recognized our plight. Pointing to a half-darkened balcony above the dining area, he said, "If you guys want to sleep up there on the floor, you can. There are blankets and it's warm!" We jumped at the invitation.

To the balcony, after eating, we adjourned. There, I grabbed a blanket and stretched out in the darkness behind a counter, out of the way, I figured. Wrong!

Tired, I quickly fell asleep, reasonably comfortable under the circumstances. Suddenly, I felt something poking me! Opening my eyes, I looked up at an elderly lady standing over me. "Young man," she said, "You're blocking the door to the ladies room," as she jabbed me with a cane.

"Sorry," I muttered as I rolled aside to let her pass, and went back to sleep.

An hour or so later, the same thing; something poking me in the ribs. And there again she stood with that cane! "Young man, you're blocking the ladies room!" she said, this time more firmly. And once more, I slid aside. Now for sure, I figured I could get some sleep.

No way! A couple hours later, still another jab, my third, in the stomach with the cane. "Young man, you're still blocking the ladies room!" my sweet, grey-haired friend snorted.

And I gave up. Clutching my blanket, I retreated to an empty easy chair, hopefully to get some rest from what little remained of the night.

Memories of snowstorms linger on. Some like my scary boyhood walk to Bertha Falk's.

Some like the one with an elderly lady, her weak kidneys, and a strong cane!

The Fairview School

It's long-gone now...the one-room country school. All that remains are memories by a handful of old-timers who, as country kids many years ago, listened for its bell to peal across the countryside each morning.

"The building used to stand right here," Morris Anderson said, waving his hand across the lush, green carpet of Lloyd Bray's clover field.

Four of us: Morris, his wife Viola, Lloyd and myself were there to reminisce; to recall days when Morris and Viola had been pupils at the Fairview School that once occupied part of what now is Bray's farm.

"The land was deeded for the school in 1905, and the school was built in 1906," Bray had told me. "The first classes were held in 1907," the Andersons added.

Morris, now 82, and Viola, a spry 77, weren't members of that first class. But they came along shortly thereafter. "I started in 1915," Morris said. "But I only went till I was thirteen. Then I had to stay home and help on the farm."

Viola attended from 1921 to 1927. "It took me only six years to complete the eight grades because I skipped third and sixth. Back in those times, they did things like that," she noted.

I asked the Andersons to describe the old school. The building was white, frame, gable-roofed, with windows along the west wall, and blackboards along the others. At the front, was an entry where coats and boots were stored. To the rear, was an attached woodshed.

"Heat came from a pot-bellied wood stove. The teacher had to build the fire each morning. Kerosene lamps mounted on wall brackets provided our light on dark days. The desks had inkwells in them," they said.

"At one time, 42 kids attended, and one teacher taught them all...reading, penmanship, arithmetic, civics, geography, language, and spelling!"

Viola well remembers the more than two-mile walk, to and from school, each morning. "In the winter, I had a mile of north wind in my face in the morning, and a mile of west wind in my face in the evening. My teacher kept a pan of snow in the entry to treat our frostbitten cheeks. We girls wore long dresses with long underwear and stockings under them, and four-buckle overshoes," she said.

"In the warm weather, I'd cut through the woods. I had a wet slough to cross that was filled with big pine logs, and I'd jump from one to another."

I asked about discipline in the old school. Morris chuckled and said, "My teacher had a pointer that worked pretty good. But behavior really wasn't a problem. We knew if we got in trouble in school, we'd be in trouble at home, too."

Yet, there were some youthful highjinks. "Once," Morris said, "one of the boys poured a can of pepper on the hot stove, and the whole school was sneezing. The teacher tried to find out who did it, but none of us would squeal."

And another time, when, as an April Fool's Day joke, Viola placed a nipple for nursing sheep on her teacher's bottle of lunch milk!

In the fall, school closed for three weeks. "Potatoes were the cash crop of the farmers," Morris explained. "And we had to help pick them."

And the end of May brought the end of the school year. "There wasn't much studying the last few days," Morris said. "Before school closed, we always cleaned the school yard. We brought tools from home, raked it and made it neat."

"Then came the school picnic. It was really a celebration! Everybody in the community came and brought grub. We visited and played games. We always had a baseball game. Even the parents got into the games."

And then it would be home to summer vacations on family farms, tending fields of potatoes, corn and rutabagas.

The Fairview School closed its doors in 1948.

Yet the other day, 43 years later, if I allowed my imagination to roam a bit, I could still hear the excited laughter of country kids, tossing beanbags and playing tag at recess, echo across Lloyd Bray's clover field.

The old school's legacy is still there. You just have to look a little harder to find it.

Music Festivals

I was poking around in the attic of my brain the other day. And there, tucked in a dim corner, amongst a bundle of frayed nerve endings, was an old memory. I picked up the faded yellowed papers and blew away the dust. There, on the cover, was a title, penned laboriously years ago by me, as a boy.

"Music Festivals," the writing said.

Ah, yes, music festivals. I'd forgotten about them. Every year about now, in spring, my country school teachers would lead us bumpkins through an annual ritual; that of exposing us to a bit of culture, to take us a tad beyond the bounds of cowbarns and cornfields.

Let me tell you, it was no easy task. Taking us, particularly us boys, away from our daydreams of baseball and marble shooting, and teaching us the difference between an alto and a soprano took some doing.

Perhaps it was because the school year was hurrying toward its end. Country grade schools, back in my boyhood, always closed well before the end of May. Perhaps that was why a fiery gleam would glow in our teacher's eye, an indication of the dedication she bore for molding us, her rag-tag charges, into a chorus capable of singing *"America, The Beautiful"* or *"Red River Valley"* with skill and fervor; enough so that we might, perhaps, win a ribbon at the county music festival.

If so, then she could close out another year of her teaching career, proud and assured that she'd imparted a touch of class, something beyond reading and writing, unto us.

So, beginning in late April, for about three weeks, there'd be the preparations and practices.

First came a sorting-out process. The twenty or so of us, had to be grouped by voice. As I recall, things would go fairly smoothly for the girls. But for us boys, voices were unpredictable. A young fellow who'd been a soprano the previous fall, might now be an alto or even a bass. And some of us were all three at the same time.

Anyway, in due time, Miss Lytle would sort us out, as best as it was possible, and arrange us into a chorus. Then, with pitch pipe firmly clenched between her lips, and arms extended like all good music conductors do, she'd put us through our practices, wheedling and scolding until out of it all emerged a reasonable facsimile of harmony.

And finally the big day, the Saturday when schools from all over the county would send their choruses, their prides and joys, to the prestigious county music festival. There, dressed in white shirts and white pants, new clothes our folks had scrimped to buy, we'd perform. . .and hopefully shower glory upon our teacher, our school, our parents.

Well, it *WAS* a big deal! We boys actually looked forward to the day with great anticipation. But not because of the singing, or the possibility of winning a blue ribbon for Miss Lytle or our beloved Hillcrest school.

The music festival, you see, was always held in a big pavilion in a county park. And the county park was situated on a lake, a lake that had fish in it. True, the morning of the festival found us boys dressed as ordered in our white shirts and pants. But in our pockets were fish lines. And inside our shirts, hidden, were tobacco cans of worms, freshly dug the night before.

Well, what happened upon our arrival at the festival is fairly obvious. Let our feet touch the ground and away we disappeared; down the mucky, muddy shore to where we could see the bluegills sunning in the shallows. And there we dallied until somehow we knew that our scheduled time to be on the program had come.

Then, back toward the pavilion we'd drift, not quite as spotlessly white as when we'd arrived. After all, one can't help a small slip, or a tiny trip, or a fat bluegill flopping on one's chest as one unhooks it.

Still, we were reasonably presentable. And since most of us boys stood in the back row, hidden by the snooty girls up front, what difference did it make?

And when Miss Lytle's pitch pipe sounded, we gave our all, our best shot. And later, if we captured a blue or a red ribbon, we were proud, even a little happy for Miss Lytle as she accepted the award.

God bless those old-time country school teachers. They showed us that there was a world out there beyond horses and haystacks.

God bless them all. . .wherever they are.

I owe them a lot.

Born in a Log Cabin

Old photographs. . .pictures from the past! Snapshots of a grandmother sitting at her spinning wheel, of an old-time, big-wheeled touring car automobile, old log buildings, a mother holding a huge northern pike, a father standing over a sheep-killing bear he'd shot.

My afternoon with Paul Kramer was coming to a close, a most pleasant few hours that I'd spent listening and looking, as he'd taken me back through time to his boyhood. And now he and his wife, Bev, were allowing me to peek at some treasured family photos in their home near Birchwood.

Over the years, I've referred to a small handful of people in this column as "true pioneers." I now add Paul Kramer to that list. Not many of us, for example, can say we were born in a log cabin. Paul Kramer can.

And he'd taken me to that birthplace; land now owned by others, on the shore of Loyhead Lake, deep in the heart of the beautifully forested, lake-speckled region of southeastern Washburn County.

"The lake is named after the man, a mining engineer, who settled here, believing that iron ore was present," Paul said. "When that failed, he decided to move on. And my father bought 120 acres of land and the buildings from him for $76.00."

"This is where I was born," Paul added, pointing to the

crumbling ruins of a stone foundation. "The building was two-storied, and made of logs. It burned many years ago. You can see the scars from the fire on that butternut tree over there."

And since his birth in 1931, Kramer's life has been spent within a few miles of that early first home, witnessing change and history as it took place around him.

He's an authority, I quickly learned. Drive the gravel roads with him, and his eyes see things that mine fail to detect. "There's where the old firelane used to go," he'd said, pointing to a faint disturbance of the earth on the forest floor.

"Stop here," he'd asked. "This is where the tin man used to stand. He was full-sized, an advertisement for a drugstore in Spooner."

Paul had mentioned earlier, an old trail that Indian people once used. And as we walked through the woods to find it, he told of his recollections.

"They'd come each fall, two or three families of men, women and children," he said. "They'd walk the trail to a marsh where they'd camp, building shelters of basswood bark, to pick wild cranberries that grew there. As a boy, I'd sit on a large rock alongside the trail, and wonder how many Indian people had passed that way."

And an old logging camp site. Dotting the forest floor were the rotting stumps of dense white pine stands, trees logged in the early 1900's. Many bore black charred wood from the forest fires that had followed the cutting of that virgin forest.

"This was probably the camp's root cellar," Paul noted, as he stood on a mound of upturned earth, now growing large trees. "At some of these camps, I've found iron shoes that the oxen wore."

Many of the lakes in the area were named by his father,

Kramer said. "This is Wolf Lake," he commented, as we passed a body of water shining blue in the afternoon sun. "Dad gave it that name after he trapped two brush wolves on it one winter."

"Bear Lake got its name because that was where Dad shot a bear that was killing our sheep. And Mason Camp Lake is named after the logging camp that was there."

What was life like for a boy growing up in the wilderness, I asked.

Summers were spent on the homeplace, helping with the work of growing corn and rutabagas on their small fields, putting up hay for their cows and a team of mules, and picking blueberries. "One year, my mother canned 122 two-quart jars," he said.

School took some family adjustments, however. As fall approached, he and his mother, sister and brother would move to Birchwood for the school year. "It was twelve miles, as the crow flies, to town from our place," he smiled.

Paul Kramer told me a lot more about those Depression-era, early-boyhood times. Of venison and fish that helped the family to survive those hard times; of finding arrowheads, when his father plowed with his big one-cylinder Mogel tractor; of a pet buck fawn that slept at the foot of his bed; of cross-country sleigh rides at Christmas, to visit grandparents.

A lot of our North Country's past lives in his memory.

Old Barns

There it stood, up ahead a quarter-mile or so, alongside the interstate. It'd caught my eye, immediately, at my first sight of it. Something about it had grabbed me, triggered long-lost memories.

An old barn.

There it stood, with dignity and grace, its backbone ridgepole still straight and true against the sky. And I stared at it intently, soaking up all the detail of its manner that I could in the less-than-the-minute's time it took the pickup to pass it by. Perhaps I'd never see it again. Something said to fix its image in my mind.

There it stood, typical of the barns built a hundred years ago, when southern Wisconsin was being settled by land-seeking immigrants from Europe. There it stood, still square on its foundation of fieldstones; raw material recycled when nearby fields had been broken by an early settler.

There it stood; now obviously empty and unused for many years, the red paint on its siding fading and graying in the face of cold rains and hot suns; siding of long, wide pine boards, lumber undoubtedly sawn from the virgin forests of northern Wisconsin that were being logged in those 1890's times, to meet the demands of a youthful, expanding America.

From the roof sprouted a row of lightning rods, fixtures

common to farm buildings of the era. And standing off to the side, partially hidden by encroaching brush and weeds, were pieces of rusting, abandoned farm machinery. Like an old hay loader, that, I'd guess, once trailed behind a creaking, wooden-wheeled farmwagon pulled by a team of feisty Belgian farmhorses, switching their tails on warm June days as windrows of alfalfa and timothy were loaded.

The old barn told a story, I decided. On it, invisible to be sure, yet unmistakably there, was a lot of me and my boyhood. And barn-watching became my pursuit for the remainder of the trip.

A turn off the interstate for a side excursion into Baraboo to visit relatives. And there, along peaceful curvy Highway 33, a veritable gold mine of picturesque old barns; handsome structures, some well-maintained, some in disrepair, with history written all over them.

There they stood. And now with my interest high, I studied them. Again, the lightning rods. But also on the roofs, are cupolas of wood and sheet metal. They're ventilators. But they're also works of art. Tributes to the barnsmiths of the day, a crowning glory to their craftsmanship.

Most of the roofs have long since been re-covered with modern-day roofing materials, asphalt shingles or rolled roofing. But occasionally there's one, sad to say, in desperate need of repair, that still has its original cedar shingles; just like those that shielded the hay mows of my grandfathers' barns when I was a boy.

Farmers, in those early times, I decided, were a compliant lot. For, the vast majority of the old barns were painted red, and still are. But, every so often, a rebel must have found his way into the neighborhood. Because there, different, would stand a barn painted white.

And silos. Look and ponder a bit, and one can find a page from the past written on the silos too. In an era of

80-acre mom-and-dad dairy farms, one silo was surely plenty. And that usually was a white concrete forty-footer. Not today. Now, it's four or more; blue steel structures so tall you can spot them a mile away.

Then, one that's a true relic. There it stood, an old-fashioned wooden-staved silo. . .it's steel bands out of kilter; sagging, leaning, cattywampuss on its fieldstone foundation. A real antique! Were it smaller, surely it would fetch a fancy price at the flea market in town.

And last, the old windmills. I have a genuine warmth in my heart for old windmills. How good a cold drink of well-water tasted on a hot August afternoon, when pulled from the depths of the earth by those whirling blades overhead.

There they stood, those old windpumps, most no longer functional; their frames draped with vine of ivy and grape, some sacrilegiously sprouting television antennas. Still, there they were, lending a touch of perpetuity to those old farm scenes.

Old barns, old silos, old windmills! They tell me stories about our past, our roots.

I like to read what they have to say. . .while they still stand.

A Gold Rush

It's an old story, one that's been told before. . .51 years ago to be exact.

But it's an interesting old tale. . .one that's spiced with the ingredients of classic mystery, things like "who-did-it" and "why'd-he-do-it." And for those reasons, it deserves to be told once more.

The strange-as-fiction events came to my attention one evening last winter, at a dinner gathering of friends. "Have you ever heard of the gold coins that were dug up years ago in the Spooner railroad yard?" one had asked.

I hadn't. Yet the question intrigued me. And in due time, it led me to Bill Falk, a retired railroad conductor. "Look up Carl Dahlgren," Bill advised. "He's the guy that found 'em!"

Recently, I sat with Dahlgren, now 76 years old, on the back porch of his neat home near Shell Lake and listened as he recounted his story.

"It was a Saturday. . .June 14, 1941. . .about 4:30 in the afternoon," Dahlgren began. "I was the cook for the bridge gang of the Omaha B and B."

The Omaha was a branch of the Chicago and Northwestern Railroad, and B and B stood for bridges and buildings, the maintenance of which was the responsibility of the crew.

"They always picked on the guy who had the least rights

to be the cook," Carl chuckled. "I had the least seniority, so I had to do the cooking."

And that quirk of fate led him to an adventure he's never forgotten.

"We had a bunk car in the railroad yard on a siding near where Lamperts Lumber now stands," he continued. "That afternoon, I had a five-gallon pail of garbage, and I went outside to bury it. I dug a hole in the sand about two feet deep, and there were those shiny pieces!"

"I didn't know what they were. I'd never seen a twenty-dollar gold piece before. They were about the size of a silver dollar. I picked up six of 'em. There was no container of any kind," he said.

Needless to say, the word of Dahlgren's discovery travelled fast. "We had two section gangs in the yard. Everybody came over and started digging," he said.

Soon townspeople joined in. "There was some wild digging going on for awhile," Carl added. "They started to undermine the tracks, and railroad officials had to put a stop to it."

In all, thirteen of the twenty-dollar coins were found. Dahlgren's six were dated to the 1870's, giving some clue as to their past.

I asked Carl what he did with those that he'd found. Gold coins had been called in a year or so earlier by the federal government.

"I never kept any of them. I turned them in to the bank," he said. "At the time I was making $5.60 a day, working six days a week. The pieces were about three weeks wages. I'd just got married the Sunday before, and I needed the money. You can spend it in a hurry when you're newly married."

Then, Bill Falk's side of the story.

"I was a sophomore in high school at the time," Bill

told me recently. "I heard the news about the gold coins. In a small town when you have a gold rush, the word gets around fast!"

To the railroad yard, he hurried.

"When I got over there, people had a big area dug up. I turned over a piece of fresh dirt, and there was a coin. It hit me right in the eye, it was that shiny. A blind man would have seen that it was gold!" he said. "I picked it up and ran for home, I was so thrilled."

And what did Falk do with his find?

"I got an offer from Chuck Trudelle of $22 for the piece, and I sold it to him," Bill told. "Then I went down to the hardware store and bought a set of golf clubs."

"Chuck had the gold piece for many years," Falk continued. "Every once in awhile he'd take it out, and we'd look at it."

Why were the coins buried? One can only speculate on the reason.

"Many people didn't believe in banks back in those days," Dahlgren said. "They were probably buried so no one would steal them."

He and Bill Falk reminisced about their gold digging the other day. It was Spooner's first and last gold rush, they agreed.

But then, who knows!

Potato Creek Country

The story begins on a bitter-cold day a winter or two ago. I'd bumped into Bert Gillette downtown. "Whew!" he said, "They'll have to bring in the grindstones tonight!"

"Bring in what?" I asked.

"The grindstones," he answered. "When it was as cold as this, years ago, the old timers always brought their grindstones into the house to keep 'em warm. So they wouldn't freeze and crack."

. . .I spent a morning recently with Bert. And again I listened to his stories, tales peppered with colorful witticisms like "tough as a boiled owl" and "wild as snake oil," as he gave me a tour of the Earl and Springbrook back-country where he grew up.

He's eighty years old now. But let me assure you, nothing has escaped his razor-sharp memory. Oh, sure, maybe he uses a cane a bit, and his hearing's needed a little help. But those things haven't slowed him down much. I found that out as I tried to lend him a hand on a hillside. No way. "I've got to get in shape for deer hunting," he promptly told me.

The morning hours melted quickly as we drove the side roads, stopping here and there, while Bert reminisced about the past. "My dad and I shot our limits of bluebills hundreds of times here," he said, pointing across the blue waters of Spooner Lake.

"One warm day I fell asleep in my blind. All of a sudden, I was awakened by shotgun blasts almost in my ear! Another hunter had sneaked in and was shooting at my decoys!"

Down the road, a mile or two, and again we paused near the lake. "Here's where we always had our summer picnics. We came by horse and wagon. And over there, in the woods, were Indian graves with their wooden shelters built over them," he told.

"As a youngster, I hunted deer all through here," he continued. "There wasn't much timber. It'd been cut... the land burned. And there weren't many deer. If you saw one fresh track in ten days, you had a good year."

And a stop alongside a patch of popple woods. "Here's where the Potato Creek Civic Center used to stand," he said. "The neighbors went together to build it. We had home talent shows, plays, dances, parties. But the bank said it wanted its money, and my dad got stuck with it."

Then, on to re-visit his old one-room Potato Creek country school, now the Anah Community Center, where Bert, at the age of five, began the first grade in 1917. And a tale of a trick he and his classmates played on their teacher; a prank so startling that she fainted dead away on the spot. "The bigger boys almost drowned her by throwing water on her," he chuckled.

The school had about thirty desks, kerosene lamps, and a big flat-topped iron stove that burned wood, he said. "We had our own hot lunch program. We took turns bringing food. We made pancakes on the stove.

"In the winter we had an ice slide over there," he said, pointing to a steep hill. "We could slide almost a quarter mile on our homemade skis and toboggans. "But we were an outlaw bunch," he added. "I remember one student, a local farm boy in his 20's, who came to school when there wasn't work on the farm, smoking a pipe, knocking the heel out of it before he came inside."

"And one April, some of us boys went skinny-dipping at noon in the creek over there across the road. But a do-gooder neighbor saw us, and we got caught."

"This was all potato country back in those days," he continued as we passed old fields, now abandoned or planted to pines. "Everything was done by hand; the planting, the cultivating, the digging. Earl and Springbrook each had four potato warehouses."

And a stop at the Gillette farm homestead where his brothers Harvey and Jack still live and grow beef cattle; where the hundred-foot-long barn, built by their father in 1913 with lumber cut from timber on the farm, with its three picturesque decorative ventilators on the roof, still stands straight and true on its foundation.

Farming wasn't the only enterprise, Bert explained. A licensed fish hatchery produced rainbow and brown trout for stocking in the small flowage nearby on Pine Brook, which flowed past the front door of the home. And downstream a short distance, was a two-acre marsh where cranberries were commercially grown.

Bert Gillette talked about a lot more; things like the old water-powered grist mill on Potato Creek, where farmers brought their grain by wagons and sleighs for grinding; of pitching bundles of oats into an old-time "thrashing machine", on the very property that's now my tree farm, of how the old settlers picked rocks until their hands bled.

Bert Gillette's witnessed a ton of our north's history.

And I thank him for sharing it with me.

Christmas Programs

Harried and hurried. . .dedicated and durable. That's the way I remember my old-time school teachers. Especially this time of the year, just before Christmas, when they were busy putting our annual Christmas programs together.

Most of us recall being part of those times, back in grade school, when we were anxious little angels with crepe-paper-covered coathanger wings, or shy little shepherds almost dying from stage fright.

What fond memories! How we treasure those moments, now in our later lives.

But what about the teachers? Those souls who were the producers, directors, costume designers, stagehands, and public relations agents for those precious productions. How did they feel? What was going on in their heads amidst all the turmoil?

Laurayne Schlief knows.

Now a young seventy-five, she and her husband, Hugh, are long retired. Laurayne taught school, most of it first grade, for thirty-eight years. And I asked her recently to tell me, from a teacher's perspective, what it was like to put on those programs each Christmas.

Teachers back in those 1930, 1940 times had to be all-everything, she said. "There were no special music or art teachers to help out. We did everything ourselves. And, of course, the basics; reading, writing and arithmetic, came first. We had to squeeze in the preparations for the programs at other times of the day."

Laurayne taught at the Hammill school, now gone, in Spooner. "Each teacher had her own program for her room back then," she noted. "Today the programs are usually school-wide."

"Every child in my class had to be in the Christmas program. That was our policy," she continued. "Everybody had to have a part. Usually we'd have a play with many characters. But with about thirty kids in my class, some ended up singing a song or reciting a poem."

"We also made the costumes ourselves, out of crepe paper and towels. We teachers stayed after school to do that."

Picking the kids to play their various parts took some doing, as it is with casting for any production. "There'd be thirty pieces to learn," she said. "I'd type those up and send them home to the mothers to teach the kids. Every day, we'd practice the parts."

The programs were always scheduled for the thursday afternoon of the week before Christmas vacation.

"That's when everything came together. The rooms would be decorated with bright paper chains and balls. Oscar Peterson, the local forest ranger, always made sure each room had a Christmas tree. And we had electric lights for it."

"But then, if a kid got sick, you had another problem, especially if the youngster was a main character in the play."

And the proud parents would arrive.

"We always tried to accommodate the parents," she told. "Sometimes they'd have youngsters in different grades, and they'd ask when their kids would be on the program. If they missed their child's part, I'd have the youngster do it again."

Funny things happened. "One year," Laurayne said, "a boy was playing a shepherd. And out front, with his parents, was his four-year-old brother. All of a sudden, the little guy walked up to the stage and said to his shepherd brother, 'what ya doin', Dickie?' That ended the program!"

And through it all, the teachers maintained their composure. "I tried not to be cross," she said. "It was supposed to be a happy time."

Laurayne Schlief told me a lot more about those old Christmas times in her classroom.

How the kids made presents for their folks, like plaster of Paris casts of their hands which they sprayed with gold paint. And silhouettes of their faces, which were pasted on pretty paper. Of candleholders, and wallpaper-covered oatmeal boxes for mothers to store their knitting in.

She told of her pupils drawing names to exchange gifts; gifts that cost a dime. Of how she always had a couple things put away in her desk to cover situations when poor youngsters couldn't afford gifts. Presents she paid for out of her own pocket.

And of how she, too, received presents from her charges, nice linen handkerchiefs, for instance. Gifts she saved, and has since many times given back to youngsters now grown. . .as remembrances of their early school days.

Christmas was a special time, she said.

"The kids liked it, and we liked it. We did our best to do our best."

Sommer's Resort

The fireplace in Elmer Sommer's living room flickered brightly, toasting the house. Through the big picture window, the scene across the frozen expanse of Sand Lake was serene; northern Wisconsin at its winter beauty best.

"I came here to Sand Lake in 1937," Sommer said to me. Sommer is 79 years old. He and his wife, Anne, have operated their resort on Sand for the past 53 years. They've seen a lot of change in that time — in the resort business, in the lake, its fishing, in the people that come to their place.

"Years ago, I had some fantastic duck hunting on the lake," he continued. "The big northern bluebills used to come in black clouds over the lake."

"Then, in the drought years of the 30's, the lake was so low, a farmer mowed that big reed bed out there with a team of horses to get forage for his cattle."

Elmer grew up in West Allis. His parents had a summer cottage on Lake Beulah in Walworth County. "I used to hang around a resort hotel on the lake. I was just a 14-year-old kid. I had a 19-foot wooden rowboat with an old 1917 Evinrude outboard motor on it, the kind you see in museums now."

"The Jesuit priests had a retreat on an island in the lake; and on Sunday mornings, I'd give people rides from the resort out there to go to Mass. I charged 25 cents a person.

That's how I got interested in the resort business.''

Sommer graduated from high school in 1930. The Great Depression had hit, "and you couldn't buy a job," he recalls. And he went to work for his father in the family grocery store. "It was all credit. Pay checks were few and far between. But people had pride, and when the books were settled years later, we only lost about $300."

"In 1937, Dad wanted me to take over the store. But my heart was in the north. Dad had provided each of us kids with $3,000 to go to college. But I told him I wanted to go up north and buy a resort. He told me he thought I was crazy, but he gave me the money."

Later that year, Sommer purchased the land and the resort he now owns, for $6,000. "That meant I had a $3,000 mortgage to pay off, a big debt in those days," he added.

"I drove up here in a used Model A truck, so overloaded with used furniture and tools, that I had thirteen blowouts on the way. I only had forty dollars in my pocket," he said.

Sommer advertised his resort, and by July, that year, had rented his five cabins. "They were just shells with kerosene lamps and kerosene stoves, outhouses and a pump. But people really had fun in them. They really appreciated their one week's vacation back then."

In 1942, with the outbreak of World War II, Elmer enlisted in the SeaBees. "Christmas Day that year found me on Guadalcanal," he remembered. "I'd hired an old fellow to stay here and take care of the resort. But he couldn't drive a car. So I bought him a donkey to go to Stone Lake with."

Two years after his discharge in 1945, Elmer married Anne. "The place was paid off, and things went a lot easier with her helping. We did all right," he said.

But times changed and the resort business began to decline. "By 1960, it was no longer a paying proposition," he said. "There used to be 85 housekeeping units on the lake. Today, there's only seven or eight left."

Sommer explains the decline very simply. "Air-conditioning did it. Years ago, people came north to escape the heat. Today, they drive all over the country in air-conditioned cars, staying in air-conditioned motels and eating in air-conditioned restaurants. Then the real estate taxes have gone up so much."

So in recent years, Sommer has been converting his cottages into recreational vehicle sites. "People rent the sites by the year, and bring their house trailers up for the summer. I've got one man who goes to Key West in the winter and comes here for the summer," he noted.

Elmer told me a lot more. Like, how he'd hurt his back in 1957 and gone into the real estate business. "I had an office in Stone Lake and did well. And I got interested in pre-built homes. I put up 148 in a ten-year period, plus several duplexes in Hayward which I still own," he said.

Then there were stories of the old days; of cutting ice from the lake to store in icehouses. Of big muskies, crappies and smallmouth bass; of highways that were just gravel roads through the woods. Tales of the slot machine days of the 1930's and of skunks in outhouses that sent ladies screaming.

Come March, Elmer and Anne will head out for their own yearly vacation. "We'll be going down to Arkansas. I'll fish for trout and play some golf," he told me.

Send me one of those little picture post cards, Elmer. One that I hope says, "Having a great time. Wish you were here!"

An Old House

"Look, Mom! I broke my arm!" I said, nonchalantly holding aloft my left arm, its wrist twisted grotesquely. I'd just fallen from the swing my dad had fashioned for me, from a rope tied to a limb of the huge burr oak that stood halfway between our house and my grandfather's blacksmith shop.

My mother had just stepped out onto the back porch of our home to shake the crumbs from the tablecloth. And upon my announcement, she turned white, almost fainting.

I was five years old. And that day, when I broke my arm, is just one of the memories I carried away from that old home, my first.

The old house stood in a grove of maples and oaks, on a gentle knoll, facing east. On a clear day, the waters of Lake Michigan laid blue on the horizon. Part of a typical farmstead, just to the south stood the other buildings; a red barn, a tall windmill with a milkhouse beside it, a machine shed, corn cribs and a pig pen.

Built probably around the turn of the century, the house was a good house by the standards of the times, the 1930's. Painted white with clapboard siding, a porch with an adjoining small "summer kitchen" off one end comprised its back side. To its front, the opposite end, facing the large lawn, was a second porch; fancier, with carved pillars and decorative woodwork. Usually it was used only when "company" came in the summer.

Inside the back door, was a large kitchen where my mother held forth, preparing meals on the old-fashioned (by today's standards) wood-fired range, beautiful in black and silver, a "reservoir" on one corner where a supply of hot water always rested. From the oven of that old stove came miracles of golden loaves of bread, spicy hams, and thick apple pies.

To one side of the kitchen laid a small pantry. There the flour and oatmeal and other staples my mother needed were stored, as well as her pots and pans. On the wall, hung a coffee grinder, a wondrous little machine. Into its round glass body, coffee beans would be poured, its crank-like handle turned, and out would spew freshly-ground, pungent-smelling coffee.

The old house had no plumbing or central-heating. Water came in pails from the windmill, and heat from the kitchen range and a pot-bellied stove in the living room. Uninsulated, the old house could get very cold in winter. Well I remember, sitting by its single-pane windows, watching, fascinated, as feathery ferns of frost formed on their panes. In the morning, the dipper might be frozen tight in the water pail.

In the evenings, after supper, the living room served as the social center. Dominating the room was the big pot-bellied heater into which chunks of wood were fed. As they burned, I'd sit, again fascinated, watching the flames flicker, listening to the grownups talk, as the kerosene lamps sent their fluttering light across the room.

Off one corner, a door led to the parlor. The parlor was rarely used, reserved for times when grandparents and aunts and uncles came to visit. The room had a special aura to it, what with the stuffed chairs and sofa along the walls, a carpet on the floor, family portraits hanging. I always had to be on my best behavior when I was in the parlor.

The house had only two bedrooms, one downstairs, one upstairs. The downstairs room was that of my folks. Furnished with a rich-looking walnut bed and a matching dresser with a large mirror, it had an elegant look. Especially the big mirror, where I could see myself.

Upstairs, in the second bedroom slept the "hired man" as he was called, a helper for my father. Sometimes there'd be more than one. Men in those depression-era times were plentiful, willing to work for little more than a place to sleep and three square meals a day.

I marvel as I contrast that old house with our home today, with its thermostatically-controlled heat, the hot and cold water that flows at a touch of a finger, the electricity that instantaneously responds to a flick of a switch.

My old house has long since disappeared.

But I'm glad I once lived there. A good part of my roots came from it.

Old houses can't live forever. . .memories can.